BODACIOUS BOOK FOR BILLIONAIRE WANNABES

BODACIOUS BOOK FOR BILLIONAIRE WANNABES

....

Valuable inspiration, insights & advice from some of the world's greatest minds & most successful people.

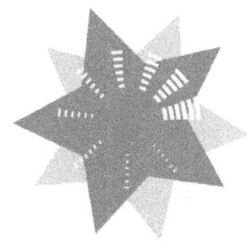

Ten-Tronck Imprint
Rob Thunder-Ten-Tronck

Copyright © 2023 by Rob Thunder-Ten-Tronck
All rights reserved.

Scripture quotations in this book are taken from the King James version of the Bible.

Bodacious Book for Billionaire Wannabes:
Valuable inspiration, insights & advice from some of the world's greatest minds & most successful people.

ISBN 978-0-943213-00-2
Library of Congress Control Number: 2022913746

Published —
Ten-Tronck
P.O. Box 3486
Martinsville, VA 24115
Email: ttronck@gmail.com

Printed in the United States of America

Book cover design by
Eddie Egesi, 2022
Interior Book Layout by
Leyda Febus, 2022

This book is to guide you when it's needed most.
— Rob Thunder-Ten-Tronck

....

DEDICATION

*To **Tom Fredell**, For your friendship, and countless visits to the Stratford festival.*

*To **Daniel Koster**, For your friendship, and thanks for the memorable visit to Alaska & Detroit Tigers baseball games.*

*To **Ernest Ephraim**, For your friendship, and your contribution to making this book possible.*

*To **Virginia Lum**, For your friendship, and your contribution to making this book possible.*

INTRODUCTION

Dear Reader,

As an entrepreneur and a business owner, you know that it is sometimes easy to get discouraged about how your enterprise is doing. I've been in this position myself, so I've created this book with hopes of keeping you, the entrepreneur or the business owner inspired, motivated and focused-- and to help you find solutions to puzzling problems. If you want to be rich and successful (or anything else that you might want to do) in the next five to ten years, read the inspirational and motivational quotes in this book to know the mindset and action plan that rich and successful people took to get where they are.

A host of sages down through the ages tell us that perseverance is the answer when you are trying to succeed in life. Yes, there will be times when things seem bad, and you can't see a way out of your predicament. However, if you persevere, you can find a solution. Sometimes, diverting your attention from the problem can help you to be open to new ways of approaching the problem. This book is meant to help you find a solution to your problem.

Note, the main purpose of this book is three-fold: 1) To inspire you, 2) to help you solve puzzling business problems and, 3) To provide guidance to help you get what you want in life.

Through quotations, this book provides you as an entrepreneur or business owner (actually it's useful to anybody who wants to succeed in life) thoughtful information, insights and advice from some of the world's greatest minds (for example, Napoleon Hill, Dr. Norman Vincent Peale, Einstein, and Socrates, etc.) and some of the world's most successful people (Bill Gates, Henry Ford, Oprah Winfrey, Elon Musk, etc.) on how to succeed in life and all other kinds of things that affect you in everyday life and how to find solutions to them. As Michel de Montaigne so famously put it "I quote others only the better to express myself."

Here is how you read this book: at the beginning read through it once, and after you have read through it once, then whenever you need a solution to a puzzling problem open the book to any page and see what wisdom is there to give you guidance.

So, whenever you're struggling to get things done, turn to these quotes for the inspiration and motivation to persevere and stay focused on what you have to do to accomplish what you want to accomplish.

....

Do you have an inspirational quote that you would like to offer to be included in the next edition, or an insightful or uplifting quote that you feel should be included? Do you want to purchase this book in bulk for promotional, educational, or business use? Do you want to purchase the subsidiary rights to this book?

If so, send your inquiry to: ttronck@gmail.com

Are you a millionaire or multi-millionaire?
Do you want to become a billionaire?

LET US COACH YOU!

Reach out with inquiries:

info@billionairewannabecoaching.com

"Ideas have no material body, but they do have consciousness, and they most certainly have will. And ideas are driven by a single impulse: to be manifested. And the only way an idea can be made manifested in our world is through collaboration with a human partner."
— *Elizabeth Gilbert*

"If you don't know where you are going, any road will get you there."
— *Lewis Carroll*

"Believe you can and you're halfway there."
— *Theodore Roosevelt*

"The value of an idea lies in the using of it."
— *Thomas A. Edison*

"If there is no struggle, there is no progress."
— *Frederick Douglass*

"Strength and growth come only through continuous effort and struggle."
— *Napoleon Hill*

"It is better to fail in originality than to succeed in imitation."
— *Herman Melville*

"Keep your face always toward to the sunshine—and shadows will fall behind you."
— *Walt Whitman*

"It's not all sunshine and rainbows, but a good amount of it actually is."
— *Unknown*

"Sunshine all the time makes a desert."
— *Arabic Proverb*

"Nothing is softer or more flexible than water, yet nothing can resist it."
— *Lao Tzu*

"The time to be happy is now, The place to be happy is here, The way to be happy is to make others so."
  — *Robert Green Ingersoll*

"Silence is more eloquent than words."
  — *Thomas Carlyle*

"To accomplish great things, we must not only act, but also dream; not only plan, but also believe."
  — *Anatole France*

"Inaction breeds doubt and fear. Action breeds confidence and courage. If you want to conquer fear, do not sit home and think about it. Go out and get busy."
  — *Dale Carnegie*

"Get busy living or get busy dying."
  — *Stephen King*

"Success is walking from failure to failure with no loss of enthusiasm."
  — *Winston Churchill*

"We need to accept that we won't always make the right decision, that we'll screw up royally sometimes – understanding that failure is not the opposite of success, it's part of success."
  — *Arianna Huffington*

"Nothing great was ever achieved without enthusiasm."
  — *Ralph Waldo Emerson*

"No person who is enthusiastic about his work has anything to fear from life."
  — *Samuel Goldwyn*

"The first step toward success is taken when you refuse to be a captive of the environment in which you first find yourself."
  — *Mark Caine*

"When one door closes, another opens; But we often look so long and regretfully upon the closed door that we do not see the one that has opened for us."
— *Alexander Graham Bell*

"When one door of happiness closes, another opens; but often we look so long at the closed door that we do not see the one which has been opened for us."
— *Helen Keller*

"When I dare to be powerful – to use my strength in the service of my vision, then it becomes less and less important whether I am afraid."
— *Audre Lorde*

"Great minds discuss ideas; average minds discuss events; small minds discuss people."
— *Eleanor Roosevelt*

"Strong minds discuss ideas, average minds discuss events, weak minds discuss people."
— *Socrates*

"A successful man is one who can lay a firm foundation with the bricks others have thrown at him."
— *David Brinkley*

"Those who dare to fail miserably can achieve greatly."
— *John F. Kennedy*

"Think of yourself as on the threshold of unparalleled success. A whole, clear, glorious life lies before you. Achieve! Achieve!"
— *Andrew Carnegie*

"To find yourself, think for yourself."
— *Socrates*

"You never know what you can do until you try."
— *William Cobbett*

"Try and fail, but don't fail to try."
— *John Quincy Adams*

"I want to be remembered as the one who tried."
— *Dr. Dorothy Height*

"You may be disappointed if you fail, but you'll be doomed if you don't try."
— *Beverly Sills*

"I can't give you a sure-fire formula for success, but I can give you a formula for failure: try to please everybody all the time."
— *Herbert Bayard Swope*

"You only live once, but if you do it right, once is enough."
— *Mae West*

"Would you like me to give you a formula for success? It's quite simple, really: Double your rate of failure. You are thinking of failure as the enemy of success. But it isn't at all. You can be discouraged by failure or you can learn from it, so go ahead and make mistakes. Make all you can. Because remember that's where you will find success."
— *Thomas J. Watson*

"It is hard to fail, but it is worse never to have tried to succeed."
— *Theodore Roosevelt*

"I'm a success today because I had a friend who believed in me and I didn't have the heart to let him down."
— *Abraham Lincoln*

"Love yourself first and everything else falls into line. You really have to love yourself to get anything done in this world."
— *Lucille Ball*

"Let us always meet each other with a smile, for the smile is the beginning of love."
— *Mother Theresa*

"A smile says, I like you. I am glad to see you."
— *Dale Carnegie*

"It's the possibility of having a dream come true that makes life interesting."
— *Paulo Coelho*

"Challenges are what make life interesting and overcoming them is what makes life meaningful."
— *Joshua J. Marine*

"One, remember to look up at the stars and not down at your feet. Two, never give up work. Work gives you meaning and purpose and life is empty without it. Three, if you are lucky enough to find love, remember it is there and don't throw it away."
— *Stephen Hawking*

"Challenges make you discover things about yourself that you never really knew."
— *Cicely Tyson*

"Don't limit your challenges, Challenge your limits."
— *Unknown*

"Love is a serious mental disease."
— *Plato*

"Our greatest fear should not be of failure… but of succeeding at things in life that don't really matter."
— *Francis Chan*

"The only person you are destined to become is the person you decide to be."
— *Ralph Waldo Emerson*

"It's fine to celebrate success but it is more important to heed the lessons of failure."
— *Bill Gates*

"Failure isn't the end of the road. It's a big red flag saying to you 'Wrong way. Turn around.'"

— *Oprah Winfrey*

"You can't let your failure define you. You have to let your failures teach you."

— *Barack Obama*

"Haste in every business brings failures."

— *Herodotus*

"Whenever you feel like a failure, just remember that even Coca Cola only sold 25 bottles their first year."

— *Unknown*

"Failure is the tuition you pay for success."

— *Walter Brunell*

"Nature does not hurry, yet everything is accomplished."

— *Lao-Tzu*

"You either create or allow everything that happens to you."

— *Jack Canfield*

"It had long since come to my attention that people of accomplishment rarely sat back and let things happen to them. They went out and happened to things."

— *Leonardo Da Vinci*

"The best way to not feel hopeless is to get up and do something. Don't wait for good things to happen to you. If you go out and make some good things happen, you will fill the world with hope, you will fill yourself with hope."

— *Barack Obama*

"Remember that the happiest people are not those getting more, but those giving more."

— *H. Jackson Brown, Jr.*

"As long as a man imagines that he cannot do a certain thing, it is impossible for him to do it."
 — *Benedict Spinoza*

"The only impossible journey is the one you never begin."
 — *Anthony Robbins*

"It is our choices, that show what we truly are, far more than our abilities."
 — *J. K. Rowling*

"Only put off until tomorrow what you are willing to die having left undone."
 — *Pablo Picasso*

"If you want to be happy, be."
 — *Count Leo Tolstoy*

"Many of life's failures are people who did not realize how close they were to success when they gave up."
 — *Thomas A. Edison*

"Most of the important things in the world have been accomplished by people who have kept on trying when there seemed to be no hope at all."
 — *Dale Carnegie*

"I always thought it was me against the world and then one day I realized it's just me against me."
 — *Kendrick Lamar*

"People in their handling of affairs often fail when they are about to succeed. If one remains as careful at the end as he was at the beginning, there will be no failure."
 — *Lao-Tzu*

"Our greatest weakness lies in giving up. The most certain way to succeed is always to try just one more time."
— *Thomas A. Edison*

"Don't be too timid and squeamish about your actions. All life is an experiment. The more experiments you make the better."
— *Ralph Waldo Emerson*

"If you want to live a happy life, tie it to a goal, not to people or things."
— *Albert Einstein*

"Very little is needed to make a happy life; it is all within yourself, in your way of thinking."
— *Marcus Aurelius*

"If you want to be happy, set a goal that commands your thoughts, liberates your energy, and inspires your hopes."
— *Andrew Carnegie*

"Success is just a war of attrition. Sure, there's an element of talent you should probably possess. But if you just stick around long enough, eventually something is going to happen."
— *Dax Shepard*

"The opposite of love is not hate; it's indifference."
— *Elie Wiesel*

"Life is ten percent what happens to you and ninety percent how you respond to it."
— *Charles Swindoll*

"The good news is that the moment you decide that what you know is more important than what you have been taught to believe, you will have shifted gears in your quest for abundance. Success comes from within, not from without."
— *Ralph Waldo Emerson*

"I never knew how to worship until I knew how to love."
— *Henry Ward Beecher*

"Those who are hardest to love need it the most."
— *Socrates*

"Dream beautiful dreams, and then work to make those dreams come true."
— *Spencer W. Kimball*

"Every great dream begins with a dreamer. Always remember, you have within you the strength, the patience, and the passion to reach for the stars to change the world."
— *Harriet Tubman*

"It is impossible to escape the impression that people commonly use false standards of measurement — that they seek power, success and wealth for themselves and admire them in others, and that they underestimate what is of true value in life."
— *Sigmund Freud*

"If we are true to ourselves, we cannot be false to anyone."
— *William Shakespeare*

"You can't have a million dollars dream on a minimum wage work ethic."
— *Unknown*

"Become a millionaire, not for the million dollars, but for what it will make of you to achieve it."
— *Jim Rohn*

"Wealth is well known to be a great comforter."
— *Plato*

"Wealth lightens not the heart and care of man."
— *Latin Proverb*

"A friend is someone who gives you total freedom to be yourself."
— *Jim Morrison*

"There is no possession more valuable than a good and faithful friend."
— *Socrates*

"To be yourself in a world that is constantly trying to make you something else is the greatest accomplishment."
— *Ralph Waldo Emerson*

"Don't flatter yourself that friendship authorizes you to say disagreeable things to your intimates. The nearer you come into relation with a person, the more necessary do tact and courtesy become."
— *Oliver Wendell Holmes*

"A little flattery will support a man through great fatigue."
— *James Monroe*

"All business is personal… Make your friends before you need them."
— *Robert L. Johnson*

"If you think someone could use a friend. Be one."
— *Unknown*

"When friendships are real, they are not glass threads or frost work, but the solidest things we can know."
— *Ralph Waldo Emerson*

"The value of a man is measured in the number of those who stand beside him, not those who follow."
— *Socrates*

"Greater love has no one than this: to lay down one's life for one's friends."
— *John 15:13*

"Most everything that you want is just outside your comfort zone."
— *Jack Canfield*

"Never let the fear of striking out keep you from playing the game."
— *Babe Ruth*

"Make your fear of losing your greatest motivator."
— *Unknown*

"If you knew who walked beside you at all times, on the path that you have chosen, you could never experience fear or doubt again."
— *Wayne Dyer*

"Life is trying things to see if they work."
— *Ray Bradbury*

"To find out what one is fitted to do and secure an opportunity to do it is the key to happiness."
— *John Dewey*

"The fruit derived from labor is the sweetest of all pleasures."
— *Luc de Clapiers*

"Every action has its pleasure and its price."
— *Socrates*

"That man is richest whose pleasures are the cheapest."
— *Henry David Thoreau*

"You will never always be motivated, so you must learn to be disciplined."
— *Unknown*

"Success in business requires training and discipline and hard work. But if you're not frightened by these things, the opportunities are just as great today as they ever were."
— *David Rockefeller*

"Discipline is not a dirty word. There is far more freedom and opportunity for creativity and success in enjoying discipline. Years ago someone I very much respect told me the reason they were successful is that they embraced doing what other people resent or are reluctant to do."

— *Janice Bryant Howroyd*

"Everything in the universe has a purpose. Indeed, the invisible intelligence that flows through everything in a purposeful fashion is also flowing through you."

— *Wayne Dyer*

"The purpose of our lives is to be happy."

— *Dalai Lama*

"Don't tell everybody your plans, instead show them your results."

— *Unknown*

"The No. 1 reason people fail in life is because they listen to their friends, family, and neighbors."

— *Napoleon Hill*

"Don't look for approval except for the consciousness of doing your best."

— *Andrew Carnegie*

"Don't let anyone convince you that your dream, your vision to be an entrepreneur, is something that you shouldn't do. What often happens is that people who are well-meaning, who really care for us, are afraid for us and talk us out of it."

— *Cathy Hughes*

"Dare to live the life you have dreamed for yourself. Go forward and make your dreams come true."

— *Ralph Waldo Emerson*

"Dreams don't work unless you do."

— *John C. Maxwell*

"There is always something about your success that displeases even your best friends."

— *Oscar Wilde*

"Short as life is, we make it still shorter by the careless waste of time."

— *Victor Hugo*

"This time, like all times, is a very good one, if we but know what to do with it."

— *Ralph Waldo Emerson*

"Life is not a spectator sport. If you're going to spend your whole life in the grandstand just watching what goes on, in my opinion, you're wasting your life."

— *Jackie Robinson*

"Your time is limited, so don't waste it living someone else's life. Don't be trapped by dogma – which is living with the results of other people's thinking."

— *Steve Jobs*

"Success is how high you bounce when you hit bottom."

— *George S. Patton*

"Before success comes in any man's life, he is sure to meet with many temporary defeats, and, perhaps, some failures. When defeats overtake a man, the easiest and most logical thing to do is to quit. That is exactly what the majority of men do."

— *Napoleon Hill*

"May you live all the days of your life."

— *Jonathan Swift*

"In three words I can sum up everything I've learned about life: It goes on."

— *Robert Frost*

"The capacity to learn is a gift, the ability to learn is a skill, the willingness to learn is a choice."
— *Brian Herbert*

"To learn something but not to do is really not to learn. To know something but not to do is really not to know."
— *Stephen Covey*

"Attitude is a choice. Happiness is a choice. Optimism is a choice. Kindness is a choice. Giving is a choice. Respect is a choice. Whatever choice you make makes you. Choose wisely."
— *Roy T. Bennet*

"Each day is an adventure in discovering the meaning of life."
— *Jack Canfield*

"Make today the day you learn something new."
— *Unknown*

"Success is not final, failure is not fatal: it is the courage to continue that counts."
— *Winston Churchill*

"Every adversity, every failure, every heartbreak, carries with it the seed of an equal or greater benefit."
— *Napoleon Hill*

"You're not obligated to win. You're obligated to keep trying. To the best you can do every day."
— *Jason Mraz*

"If life were predictable it would cease to be life, and be without flavor."
— *Eleanor Roosevelt*

"It is better to light a candle than curse the darkness."
— *Eleanor Roosevelt*

"If you don't design your own life plan, chances are you'll fall into someone else's plan. And guess what they have planned for you? Not much."

— *Jim Rohn*

"Be a first-rate version of yourself, not a second-rate version of someone else."

— *Judy Garland*

"The secrets of this earth are not for all men to see, but only for those who will seek them."

— *Ayn Rand*

"The question isn't who is going to let me; it's who is going to stop me."

— *Ayn Rand*

"Passion is a feeling that tells you: this is the right thing to do. Nothing can stand in my way. It doesn't matter what anyone else says. This feeling is so good that it cannot be ignored. I'm going to follow my bliss and act upon this glorious sensation of joy."

— *Wayne Dyer*

"I can and I will. Watch me."

— *Carrie Green*

"The three great essentials to achieve anything worthwhile are, first, hard work; second, stick-to-itiveness; third, common sense."

— *Thomas A. Edison*

"Common sense is that which judges the things given to it by other senses."

— *Leonardo da Vinci*

"Flaming enthusiasm backed up by horse sense and persistence is the quality that most frequently makes for success."

— *Dale Carnegie*

"I never dreamt of success. I worked for it."
— *Estee Lauder*

"Continuous effort — not strength or intelligence — is the key to unlocking our potential."
— *Liane Cardes*

"A surplus of effort could overcome a deficit of confidence."
— *Sonia Sotomayer*

"To uncover your true potential, you must first find your own limits and then you have to have the courage to blow past them."
— *Picabo Street*

"One of the main reasons why most people don't get what they want is they haven't decided what they want. They haven't defined their desires in clear and compelling detail."
— *Jack Canfield*

"When your desires are strong enough, you will appear to possess superhuman powers to achieve."
— *Napoleon Hill*

"Dreams are lovely but they are just dreams. Fleeting, ephemeral, pretty. But dreams do not come true just because you dream them. It's hard work that makes things happen. It's hard work that creates change."
— *Shonda Rhimes*

"I learned this, at least, by my experiment: that if one advances confidently in the direction of his dreams, and endeavors to live the life which he has imagined, he will meet with a success unexpected in common hours."
— *William David Thoreau*

"The successful warrior is the average man, with laser-like focus."
— *Bruce Lee*

"A man is a success if he gets up in the morning and gets to bed at night, and in between he does what he wants to do."
— *Bob Dylan*

"Yesterday is history, tomorrow is a mystery, today is a gift of God, which is why we call it the present."
— *Bill Keane*

"We cannot overstate our debt to the past, but the moment has the supreme claim."
— *Ralph Waldo Emerson*

"Life isn't about finding yourself. Life is about creating yourself."
— *George Bernard Shaw*

"Mastering others is strength. Mastering yourself is true power."
— *Lao-Tzu*

"The whole secret of a successful life is to find out what is one's destiny to do, and then do it."
— *Henry Ford*

"The big secret in life is that there is no big secret. Whatever your goal, you can get there if you're willing to work."
— *Oprah Winfrey*

"And here is the prime condition of success, the great secret. Concentrate your energy, thoughts and capital exclusively upon the business in which you are engaged in. Having begun in one line, resolve to fight it out on that line; to lead in it. Adopt every improvement, have the best machinery and know the most about it."
— *Andrew Carnegie*

"The sum of wisdom is that time is never lost that is devoted to work."
— *Ralph Waldo Emerson*

"True wisdom comes to each of us when we realize how little we understand about life, ourselves, and the world around us."
— *Socrates*

"Success? I don't know what that word means. I'm happy. But success, that goes back to what in somebody's eyes success means. For me, success is inner peace. That's a good day for me."
— *Denzel Washington*

"You miss 100 percent of the shots you never take."
— *Wayne Gretzky*

"Life itself is the most wonderful fairy tale."
— *Hans Christian Andersen*

"The greater danger for most of us is not that our aim is too high and we miss it, but that it is too low and we reach it."
— *Michelangelo*

"Do not go where the path may lead; go instead where there is no path and leave a trail."
— *Ralph Waldo Emerson*

"Success is the sum of small efforts repeated day in and day out."
— *Robert Collier*

"We become what we repeatedly do."
— *Stephen Covey*

"We are what we repeatedly do; excellence, then, is not an act but a habit."
— *Aristotle*

"We know what we are, but know not what we may be."
— *William Shakespeare*

"The big lesson in life, baby, is never be scared of anyone or anything."
— *Frank Sinatra*

"If you aren't going all the way, why go at all?"
— *Joe Namath*

"To love and be loved is to feel the sun from both sides."
— *David Viscott*

"At the touch of love, everyone becomes a poet."
— *Plato*

"Love is an irresistible desire to be irresistibly desired."
— *Robert Frost*

"The deepest desire of the human spirit is to be acknowledged."
— *Stephen Covey*

"The person who reads too much and uses his brain too little will fall into lazy habits of thinking."
— *Albert Einstein*

"Good or bad, habits always deliver results."
— *Jack Canfield*

"What we steadily, consciously, habitually think we are, that we tend to become."
— *John Cowper Powys*

"Before you can become a millionaire, you must learn to think like one."
— *Thomas J. Stanley*

"People don't decide their future, they decide their habits and their habits decide their future."
— *F. M. Alexander*

"To change bad habits, we must study the habits of successful role models."
— *Jack Canfield*

"Motivation may be what starts you off, but it's habit that keeps you going back for more."
— *Miya Yamanouch*

"Life would be tragic if it weren't funny."
— *Stephen Hawking*

"Better to have loved and lost, than to have never loved at all."
— *St. Augustine*

"Every child is an artist, the problem is staying an artist when you grow up."
— *Pablo Picasso*

"Have no fear of perfection, you'll never reach it."
— *Salvador Dali*

"Life is not a problem to be solved, but a reality to be experienced."
— *Soren Kierkegaard*

"Life is not a problem to be solved, but a mystery to be lived."
— *Unknown*

"Every time you think the problem is out there, that very thought is the problem."
— *Stephen Covey*

"Curiosity about life in all of its aspects, I think, is still the secret of great creative people."
— *Leo Burnett*

"Imagination is the beginning of creation. You imagine what you desire, you will create what you imagine, and at last, you create what you will."
— *George Bernard Shaw*

"The journey of a thousand miles begins with one step."
— *Lao Tzu*

"Imagination was given to man to compensate him for what he is not, and a sense of humor was provided to console him for what he is."
— *Oscar Wilde*

"What you do speaks so loudly that I cannot hear what you say."
— *Ralph Waldo Emerson*

"Spread love everywhere you go: first of all in your own house. Give love to your children, to your wife or husband, to a next door neighbor. Let no one ever come to you without leaving better and happier. Be the living expression of God's kindness; kindness in your face, kindness in your eyes, kindness in your smile, kindness in your warm greeting."
— *Mother Theresa*

"Be happy for this moment. This moment is your life."
— *Omar Khayyam*

"Human behavior flows from three main sources: desire, emotion and knowledge."
— *Plato*

"Every human has four endowments – self-awareness, conscience, independent will and creative imagination. These give us the ultimate human freedom… The power to choose, to respond, to change."
— *Stephen Covey*

"The secret of change is to focus all of your energy not on fighting the old, but on building the new."
— *Socrates*

"Be the change you want to see in the world."
— *Mahatma Gandhi*

"The best way out is always through."
— *Robert Frost*

"The dream crossed twilight between birth and dying."
— *T. S. Eliot*

"People are just as happy as they make up their minds to be."
— *Abraham Lincoln*

"Don't think. Thinking is the enemy of creativity. It's self-conscious, and anything self-conscious is lousy. You can't try to do things. You simply must do things."
— *Ray Bradbury*

"Creativity is just connecting things. When you ask creative people how they did something, they feel a little guilty because they didn't really do it, they just saw something. It seemed obvious to them after a while."
— *Steve Jobs*

"Sing like no one's listening, love like you've never been hurt, dance like nobody's watching, and live like its heaven on earth."
— *Mark Twain*

"Heaven is a state of mind, not a location."
— *Wayne Dyer*

"The power of imagination makes us infinite."
— *John Muir*

"Imagination is a very high sort of seeing."
— *Ralph Waldo Emerson*

"If you do not see great riches in your imagination, you will never see them in your bank balance."
— *Napoleon Hill*

"Live out of your imagination, not your history."
— *Stephen Covey*

"Each experience in your life was absolutely necessary in order to have gotten you to the next place, and the next place, up to this very moment."
— *Wayne Dyer*

"Doing the best at this moment puts you in the best place for the next moment."
— *Oprah Winfrey*

"All we can do is the best we can do."
— *David Axelrod*

"Good. Better. Best. Never let it rest. Til your good is better and your better is best."
— *St. Jerome*

"What is coming is better than what is gone."
— *Unknown*

"Originality is nothing but judicious imitation."
— *Voltaire*

"Life is made of ever so many partings welded together."
— *Charles Dickens*

"Love is like the wind, you can't see it, but you can feel it."
— *Nicholas Sparks*

"Every man I meet is my superior in some way. In that, I learn of him."
— *Ralph Waldo Emerson*

"All men are by nature equal, made all of the same earth by one Workman; and, however, we deceive ourselves, as dear unto God is the poor peasant as the mighty prince."
— *Plato*

"I shall pass this way but once; any good, therefore, that I can do or any kindness that I can show to any human being, let me do it now. Let me not defer nor neglect it, for I shall not pass this way again."
— *Unknown*

"When people tell me they've learned from experience, I tell them the trick is to learn from other people's experience."
— *Warren Buffett*

"Life is not what you alone make it. Life is the input of everyone who touched your life and every experience that entered it. We are all part of one another."
— *Yuri Kochiyama*

"Believing in yourself is a choice. It's an attitude you develop over time."
— *Jack Canfield*

"Happiness is by choice…not by chance."
— *Unknown*

"Happiness doesn't depend on any external conditions, it is governed by our mental attitude."
— *Dale Carnegie*

"We are the creative force of our life, and through our own decisions rather than our conditions, if we carefully learn to do certain things, we can accomplish those goals."
— *Stephen Covey*

"Remember, no human condition is ever permanent."
— *Socrates*

"The true measure of success is determined by your home life."
— *Dan Black*

"Be an encourager. The world has plenty of critics already."
— *Dave Willis*

"Be an Encourager. When you encourage others, you boost their self-esteem, enhance their self-confidence, make them work harder, lift their spirits and make them successful in their endeavors. Encouragement goes straight to the heart and is always available. Be an encourager. Always."
— *Roy T. Bennett*

"Our chief want in life is someone who shall make us do what we can."
— *Ralph Waldo Emerson*

"Just as food eaten without appetite is a tedious nourishment, so does study without zeal damage the memory by not assimilating what it absorbs."
— *Leonardo da Vinci*

"Life is a tedious process of learning we are fools."
— *George Meredith*

"The only true wisdom is to know that you know nothing."
— *Socrates*

"When we know ourselves fools, we are already something better"
— *George Meredith*

"It's not what happens to you but how you react to it that matters."
— *Epictetus*

"Every problem contains the seeds of its own solution."
— *Stanley Arnold*

"A man is not idle because he is absorbed in thought. There is a visible labor and there is an invisible labor."
— *Victor Hugo*

"The soul becomes dyed with the color of its thoughts."
— *Marcus Aurelius*

"This is the final test of a gentleman: his respect for those who can be of no possible service to him."
— *William Lyon Phelps*

"If there be truer measure of a man than by what he does, it must be by what he gives."
— *Robert South*

"The measure of a man is what he does with power."
— *Plato*

"We are to add what we can to life, not to get what we can from it."
— *William Osler*

"Even if I knew certainly that the world would end tomorrow, I would plant a tree today."
— *Martin Luther*

"Two are better than one, because they have a good return for their labor: If either of them falls down, one can help the other up. But pity anyone who falls and has no one to help them up. Also, if two lie down together, they will keep warm. But how can one keep warm alone?"
— *Ecclesiastes 4:9-11*

"Though one may be overpowered, two can defend themselves. A cord of three strands is not quickly broken."
— *Ecclesiastes 4:12*

"We have forty million reasons for failure, but not a single excuse."
— *Rudyard Kipling*

"Show me a thoroughly satisfied man and I will show you a failure."
— *Thomas A. Edison*

"What can't be cured must be endured."
— *Fyodor Dostoyevsky*

"I affirm to you the tremendous potential you have, not beyond anything you could ever imagine."

— *Stephen Covey*

"Be strong enough to let go and wise enough to wait for what you deserve."

— *Unknown*

"When the pain of an obstacle is too great, challenge yourself to be stronger."

— *Unknown*

"Just as we develop our physical muscles through overcoming opposition – such as lifting weights – we develop our character muscles by overcoming challenges and adversity."

— *Stephen Covey*

"At the end of the day we can endure much more than we think we can."

— *Frida Kahlo*

"Do not spoil what you have by desiring what you have not; remember that what you now have was once among the things you only hoped for."

— *Epicurus*

"The bad news is that time flies. The good news is you are the pilot."

— *Michael Altshuler*

"You can think your way into or out of almost any circumstance, good or bad."

— *Napoleon Hill*

"There is nothing either good or bad, but thinking makes it so."

— *William Shakespeare*

"The only difference between a rich person and a poor person is how they use their time."
    — *Robert Kiyosaki*

"He is rich who owns the day, and no one owns the day who allows it to be invaded with fret and anxiety."
    — *Ralph Waldo Emerson*

"Nothing in the affairs of men is worthy of great anxiety."
    — *Plato*

"It's never about your resources; it's about your resourcefulness."
    — *Anthony Robbins*

"It is the mind that makes the body rich."
    — *Andrew Carnegie*

"The mind is everything; what you think you become."
    — *Socrates*

"Life's too short to hang out with people who aren't resourceful."
    — *Jeff Bezos*

"One thing for sure, if you don't play, you don't win."
    — *Kylie Francis*

"I win or I learn, but I never lose."
    — *Unknown*

"You were born to win, but to be a winner, you must plan to win, prepare to win, and expect to win."
    — *Zig Ziglar*

"Whatever you do never run back to what broke you."
    — *Frank Ocean*

"How you respond to the challenge in the second half will determine what you become after the game, whether you are a winner or a loser."
— *Lou Holtz*

"Always imitate the behavior of the winner when you lose."
— *George Meredith*

"A winner is a dreamer who never gives up."
— *Nelson Mandela*

"When one side benefits more than the other, that's a win-lose situation. To the winner it might look like success for a while, but in the long run, it breeds resentment and distrust."
— *Stephen Covey*

"Quitters never win. Winners never quit!"
— *Dr. Irene C. Kassorla*

"A man is not finished when he is defeated. He is finished when he quits."
— *Richard Nixon*

"When you win, say nothing, when you lose, say less."
— *Paul Brown*

"When I win and when I lose, I take ownership of it, because I really am in charge of what I do."
— *Nicki Mina*

"If you are possessed by an idea, you find it expressed everywhere, you even smell it."
— *Thomas Mann*

"Any idea, plan, or purpose may be placed in the mind through repetition of thought."
— *Napoleon Hill*

"When Plan "A" doesn't work, don't worry, you still have 25 more letters to go through."
— *Unknown*

"A dream (something that you truly want to accomplish) is a wish your heart makes."
— *Cinderella*

"Wherever you go, go with all your heart."
— *Confucius*

"We don't see things as they are, we see things as we are."
— *Anais Nin*

"We see the world not as it is, but as we are."
— *Stephen Covey*

"If you argue for your limitations, you get to keep them."
— *Unknown*

"Never be limited by other people's limited imaginations."
— *Mae Jemison*

"I am realistic - I expect miracles."
— *Wayne Dyer*

"The fact is that when anyone starts expecting a miracle, he presently becomes so conditioned in mind that he begins actually making miracles happen."
— *Dr. Norman Vincent Peale*

"Always remember that to every disadvantage there is a corresponding advantage."
— *W. Clement Stone*

"If you are looking for a big opportunity, seek out a big problem."
— *Unknown*

"There is a soft spot in every problem. All you got to do is keep looking until you find it."
— *Harlow B. Andrews.*

"Do the best you can until you know better. Then when you know better, do better."
— *Maya Angelou*

"Do what you can, with what you have, where you are."
— *Theodore Roosevelt*

"The ancestor of every action is a thought."
— *Ralph Waldo Emerson*

"Knowing something doesn't change your life. Doing something does."
— *Marie Forleo*

"You must become the producer, director and actor in the unfolding story of your life."
— *Wayne Dyer*

"Once you embrace unpleasant news, not as a negative but as evidence of a need for change, you aren't defeated by it."
— *Bill Gates*

"Whether you think you can or you think you can't, you're right."
— *Henry Ford*

"If you bring forth what is within you, what you bring forth will save you, if you do not bring forth what is within you, what you do not bring forth will destroy you."
— *Gospel of Thomas*

"Pray about your goal to be sure it is right, because if it is not right, it is wrong, and nothing wrong ever turned out right."
— *Dr. Norman Vincent Peale*

"The obvious is that which is never seen until someone expresses it simply."
— *Kablil Gibran*

"Great successes never come without risk."
— *Flavius Josephus*

"If you don't risk anything, you risk even more."
— *Erica Jong*

"The biggest risk is not taking any risk. In a world that is changing really quickly, the only strategy that is guaranteed to fail is not taking risks."
— *Mark Zuckerberg*

"Take calculated risks. That is quite different from being rash."
— *George S. Patton*

"Take the risk or lose the chance."
— *Unknown*

"It's easy to attack and destroy an act of creation. It's a lot more difficult to perform one."
— *Chuck Palahniuk*

"A non-doer is very often a critic, that is, someone who sits back and watches doers, and then waxes philosophically about how the doers are doing. It's easy to be a critic, but being a doer requires effort, risk, and change."
— *Wayne Dyer*

"In a world where there is so much to be done, I felt strongly impressed that there must be something for me to do."
— *Dorothy Dix*

"Most people give up just when they're about to achieve success. They quit on the one-yard line. They give up at the last minute of the game one foot from a winning touchdown."
— *Ross Perot*

"Your only limit is your mind."
— *Unknown*

"You can do anything you set your mind to."
— *Benjamin Franklin*

"We can do anything we want to do if we stick to it long enough."
— *Helen Keller*

"There is one grand lie -- that we are limited. The only limits we have are the limits we believe."
— *Wayne Dyer*

"Don't give up, don't take anything personally, and don't take no for an answer."
— *Sophia Amoruso*

"Just don't give up trying to do what you really want to do. If there is love and inspiration, I don't think you can go wrong."
— *Ella Fitzgerald*

"A walk to a nearby park may give you more energy and inspiration in life than spending two hours in front of a screen."
— *Tsang Lindsay*

"Small opportunities are often the beginning of great enterprises."
— *Demosthenes*

"The beginning is the most important part of the work."
— *Plato*

"Your most important work is always ahead of you, never behind you."
— *Stephen Covey*

"Self-trust is the first secret of success."
— *Ralph Waldo Emerson*

"Never give up! Failure and rejection are only the first step to succeeding."
— *Unknown*

"There's a four-letter word you must use when you get rejected….next."
— *Jack Canfield*

"Don't be upset when people reject you. Nice things are rejected all the time by people who can't afford them."
— *Unknown*

"Men are born to succeed not to fail."
— *Henry Thoreau*

"Never let your head hang down. Never give up and sit down and grieve. Find another way."
— *Satchel Paige*

"Believe in yourself, take on your challenges, dig deep within yourself to conquer fears. Never let anyone bring you down. You got to keep going."
— *Chantal Sutherland*

"Come at a problem a different way if the methodology you are using is not working. And if the new approach fails to go well, then come at it still another way until you do find the key to the situation. For there is a key, there always is, and continual, thoughtful, undeviating search and attack will produce it."
— *Dr. Norman Vincent Peale*

"Alone we can do so little. Together we can do so much."
— *Helen Keller*

"If something is important enough, or you believe something is important enough, even if you are scared, you will keep going."
— *Elon Musk*

"You must do the things you think you cannot do."
— *Eleanor Roosevelt*

"Those who cannot change their minds cannot change anything."
— *George Bernard Shaw*

"Dreams are the seeds of change. Nothing grows without a seed, and nothing ever changes without a dream."
— *Debby Boone*

"You can't go back and change the beginning, but you can start where you are and change the ending."
— *C.S. Lewis*

"If we keep doing what we're doing, we're going to keep getting what we're getting."
— *Stephen Covey*

"No action is too small when it comes to changing the world… I'm inspired every time I meet an entrepreneur who is succeeding against all odds."
— *Cyril Ramaphosa*

"If you think you're too small to make a difference, try sleeping with a mosquito."
— *Dalai Lama*

"Knowledge, if it does not determine action, is dead to us."
— *Plotinus*

"Knowledge is true opinion."
— *Plato*

"What, then, shall we say in response to these things? If God is for us, who can be against us?"
— *Romans 8:31*

"Learn from the mistakes of others. You can't live long enough to make them all yourself."
— *Eleanor Roosevelt*

"Do not be embarrassed by your failures, learn from them and start again."
— *Sir. Richard Branson*

"If you want to go fast, go alone; if you want to go far go together"
— *African Proverb*

"The man who goes alone can start today; but he who travels with another must wait until that other person is ready."
— *Henry David Thoreau*

"Innovation is the specific instrument of entrepreneurship...the act that endows resources with a new capacity to create wealth."
— *Peter Drucker*

"The capitalist system does not guarantee that everybody will become rich, but it guarantees that anybody can become rich."
— *Raul R. deSales*

"A man is rich in proportion to the number of things he can afford to let alone."
— *Henry David Thoreau*

"It's not your salary that makes you rich, it's your spending habits."
— *Charles A. Jaffe*

"The easiest way to remain poor is to pretend to be rich."
— *Unknown*

"You have to do it by yourself, and you can't do it alone."
— *Martin Rutte*

"Nothing in this world always can take place of persistence; persistence and determination alone are omnipotent."
— *Calvin Coolidge*

"Success seems to be largely a matter of hanging on after others have let go."
— *William Feather*

"Never despair, but if you do, work on in despair."
— *Edmund Burke*

"Dare and the world always yield. Or, if it beats you sometimes, dare again, and it will succumb."
— *William Makepeace*

"Show me a guy who's afraid to look bad, and I'll show you a guy you can beat every time."
— *Lou Brock*

"Words can inspire, thoughts can provoke, but only action truly brings you closer to your dreams."
— *Brad Sugars*

"Action is the foundational key to all success."
— *Pablo Picasso*

"Perseverance is the foundation of all action."
— *Lao Tzu*

"All I have seen teaches me to trust the creator for all I have not seen."
— *Ralph Waldo Emerson*

"Nothing ever goes away until it teaches us what we need to know."
— *Pema Chodron*

"God is with those who perseveres"
> — *Mohammed*

"Victory belongs to the most persevering."
> — *Napoleon Bonaparte*

"Victories that are easy are cheap. Those only worth having come as the result of hard fighting."
> — *Henry Ward Beecher*

"There is some good in the world, and it's worth fighting for."
> — *J.R.R. Tolkien*

"Victory is always possible for the person who refuses to stop fighting."
> — *Napoleon Hill*

"What counts is not necessarily the size of the dog in the fight- it's the size of the fight in the dog."
> — *Dwight D. Eisenhower*

"Courage and perseverance have a magical talisman, before which difficulties disappear and obstacles vanish into air."
> — *John Quincy Adams*

"Courage is knowing what not to fear."
> — *Plato*

"Men fail much often from want of perseverance than from want of talent."
> — *William Cobbett*

"Never think that God's delays are God's denials. Hold on; hold fast; hold out. Patience is genius."
> — *Count de Buffon*

"Adopt the pace of nature: her secret is patience."
> — *Ralph Waldo Emerson*

"The impatient idealist says: 'Give me a place to stand and I shall move the earth.' But such a place does not exist. We all have to stand on the earth itself and go with her at her pace."
— *Chinua Achebe*

"Be patient and calm; no one can catch a fish with anger."
— *Herbert Hoover*

"Never rule out a goal because you think it's unattainable. Be audacious."
—; *Ray Dallo*

"I think frugality drives innovation, just like other constraints do. One of the only ways to get out of a tight box is to invent your way out."
— *Jeff Bezos*

"Patience and time do more than force and rage."
— *Jean deLaFontaine*

"Patience has its limits. Take it too far and it's cowardice."
— *George Jackson*

"Go confidently in the direction of your dreams. Live the life you have imagined."
— *Henry David Thoreau*

"If you don't build your dreams, someone else will hire you to help build theirs."
— *Dhirubhai Ambani*

"People who don't have goals, work for people who do."
— *Jack Canfield*

"Being confident and believing in your own self-worth is necessary to achieving your potential."
— *Sheryl Sandberg*

"If you can imagine it, you can achieve it. If you can dream it, you can become it."

— *Unknown*

"The only thing standing in the way between you and your goal is the BS story you keep telling yourself as to why you can't achieve it."

— *Jordan Belfort*

"When you want something, all the universe conspires in helping you achieve it."

— *Paulo Coelho*

"The more you see yourself as what you'd like to become, and act as if what you want is already there, the more you'll activate those dormant forces that will collaborate to transform your dream into your reality."

— *Wayne Dyer*

"Failure is a feeling long before it's an actual result."

— *Michelle Obama*

"A goal is a dream with a deadline."

— *Napoleon Hill*

"Give your goal complete and unremitting effort, and never give up trying--and apply positive thinking."

— *Dr. Norman Vincent Peale*

"I love those who can smile in trouble, who can gather strength from distress, and grow brave by reflection. 'Tis the business of little minds to shrink, but they whose heart is firm, and whose conscience approves their conduct, will pursue their principles unto death."

— *Leonardo da Vinci*

"Your positive action combined with positive thinking results in success."

— *Shiv Khera*

"Think about where you want to get in life. Come to a firm decision about your basic objective. Formulate and write your goals in a sharp, clear statement, and eliminate all fuzziness of thought."
— *Dr. Norman Vincent Peale*

"Clarify your purpose. What is the why behind everything you do. When we know this in life or design it is very empowering and the path is clear."
— *Jack Canfield*

"Five days a week, I read my goals before I go to sleep and when I wake up. There are 10 goals around health, family, and business with expiration dates, and I update them every six months."
— *Daymond John*

"It's a universal principle that you get more of what you think about, talk about, and feel strongly about."
— *Jack Canfield*

"Whoever makes a fortune by a lying tongue is chasing a bubble over deadly snares."
— *Proverb 21:6*

"If we tried to think of a good idea, we wouldn't have been able to think of a good idea. You just have to find the solution for a problem in your own life."
— *Brian Chesky*

"Whatever you are, be a good one."
— *Abraham Lincoln*

"Do the best you can. No one can do more than that."
— *John Wooden*

"You have to be open to new ideas and new ways of doing things if you want break throughs in your life."
— *Gary Keller*

"It is only through a human's efforts that an idea can be escorted out of the ether and into the realm of the actual."
    — *Elizabeth Gilbert*

"All achievements, all earned riches have their beginning in an idea."
    — *Andrew Carnegie*

"The starting point of all achievement is desire. Keep this constantly in mind. Weak desires bring weak results, just as a small fire makes a small amount of heat."
    — *Napoleon Hill*

"Ideas are easy. Implementation is hard."
    — *Guy Kawasaki*

"A scoundrel, a villain, is he who deals in crooked talk."
    — *Proverb 6:12*

"A crooked course is the longest road to take to get anywhere."
    — *B.C. Forbes*

"The individual activity of one man with backbone will do more than a thousand men with a mere wishbone."
    — *J.H. Boetcher*

"The greatest remedy for anger is delay."
    — *Seneca*

"Employ your time in improving yourself by other men's writings so that you shall come easily by what others have labored hard for."
    — *Socrates*

"Man needs difficulties; they are necessary for health."
    — *Carl Jung*

"One does not discover new lands without consenting to lose sight of the shore for a very long time."
    — *Andre Gide*

"Don't let small things cut your life down to size. Think big, aim high, act bold. And see just how big you can blow up your life."
— *Gary Keller*

"Aim for the highest."
— *Andrew Carnegie*

"In the long run men hit only what they aim at. Therefore, though they fail immediately, they had better aim at something high."
— *Henry David Thoreau*

"We aim above the mark to hit the mark."
— *Ralph Waldo Emerson*

"Make no little plans; they have no magic to stir men's blood. Make big plans, aim high in hope and work."
— *Daniel H. Burnham*

"To travel hopefully is better than to arrive."
— *James Jeans*

"The first wealth is health."
— *Ralph Waldo Emerson*

"Wealth consists not in having great possessions, but in having few wants."
— *Epictetus*

"He who has health has hope, and he who has hope has everything."
— *Arabian Proverb*

"Attention to health is life's greatest hindrance."
— *Plato*

"Life is a grindstone; whether it grinds you down or polishes you depends on what you're made of."
— *Jacob M. Braude*

"Life is not fair, get used to it."
— *Bill Gates*

"You will never do anything in this world without courage. It is the greatest quality of the mind next to honor."
— *Aristotle*

"When you have a problem, one that is especially difficult and baffling, perhaps terribly discouraging, there is one basic principle to apply and keep on applying. It is simply this---never quit."
— *Dr. Norman Vincent Peale*

"The greatest ability in business is to get along with others and influence their actions."
— *John Hancock*

"They are able because they think they are able."
— *Virgil*

"Executive ability is deciding quickly and getting somebody else to do the work."
— *John G. Pollard*

"To accomplish great things, we must dream as well as act."
— *Anatole France*

"Who begins too much accomplishes little."
— *German Proverb*

"It's amazing what you can accomplish if you do not care who gets the credit."
— *Harry S. Truman*

"The way to get things done is not to mind who gets the credit for doing them."
— *Benjamin Jewett*

"The secret of success lies not in doing your own work but in recognizing the best person to do it."
> — *Andrew Carnegie*

"Every calling is great when greatly pursued."
> — *Oliver Wendell Holmes*

"Don't let what you cannot do interfere with what you can do."
> — *John Wooden*

"In difficult situations the boldest plans are the safest."
> — *Titus Livy*

"When you cannot make up your mind which of two evenly balanced courses of action you should take—chose the bolder."
> — *W.J. Slim*

"There is no such thing as a great talent without great willpower."
> — *Unknown*

"Behold the turtle. He makes progress only when he sticks his neck out."
> — *James B. Conant*

"Lose no time; be always employed in something useful."
> — *Benjamin Franklin*

"An investment in knowledge pays the best interest."
> — *Benjamin Franklin*

"Life reflects your own thoughts back to you."
> — *Napoleon Hill*

"The actions of men are the best interpreters of their thoughts."
> — *John Lock*

"If it's to be, it's up to me."
> — *William Johnsen*

"Taking complete ownership of your outcomes by holding no one but yourself responsible for them is the most powerful thing you can do to drive your success."
— *Gary Keller*

"Build momentum by accumulating small successes."
— *Unknown*

"The average person puts only 25% of his energy and ability into his work. The world will take off its hat to those who put in more than 50% of their capacity and the world will stand on its head for those few and far between souls who devote 100%."
— *Andrew Carnegie*

"To achieve major success in life, you must accept 100% responsibility for your life and results. Nothing less will do."
— *Jack Canfield*

"Big jobs usually go to the men who prove their ability to outgrow small ones."
— *Ralph Waldo Emerson*

"The diamond cannot be polished without friction, nor the man perfected without trials."
— *Chinese Proverb*

"What I must do is all that concerns me, not what the people think."
— *Ralph Waldo Emerson*

"Open my heart, Lord, to choose peace in the midst of small inconveniences and major concerns."
— *Lynne Hartke*

"Let nothing trouble you; let nothing frighten you; everything changes but God does not. Through patience you will obtain everything; whoever has God lacks nothing, having God is enough."
— *St. Teresa of Avila*

"Let go of doubts and start believing that you can do whatever it is you set out to do."
— *Jack Canfield*

"Change is painful, but nothing is as painful as staying stuck somewhere you don't belong."
— *Mandy Hale*

"There are only two sources of human vice, idles and superstition; and only two virtues, energy and intelligence."
— *Count Leo Tolstoy*

"We don't love men so much for the good they have done us, as for the good we have done them."
— *Sterne*

"A healthy condition in the body and the mind is the basic value to all of life's living."
— *John Amos Banks*

"Money can't buy happiness, but it can make you awfully comfortable while you're being
miserable."
— *Clare Booth Luce*

"Man finds his lasting happiness only in God."
— *Blaise Pascal*

"He who guards his mouth and his tongue keeps himself from trouble."
— *Proverbs 21:23*

"The relationship between commitment and doubt is by no means an antagonistic one."
— *Rollo May*

"Doubt kills more dreams than failure ever will."
— *Suzy Kassem*

"Whenever you find yourself doubting how far you can go, just remember how far you have come."
   — *Unknown*

"Conviction is worthless unless it is converted into conduct."
   — *Thomas Carlyle*

"The highest Court is in the end one's own conscience."
   — *Max Planck*

"The longer you hang in there, the greater the chance that something will happen in your favor. No matter how hard it seems, the longer you persist, the more likely your success."
   — *Jack Canfield*

"Keep on going, and the chances are that you will stumble on something, perhaps when you are least expecting it. I never heard of anyone ever stumbling on something sitting down."
   — *Charles F Kettering*

"Take a chance! All life is a chance. The man who goes furthest is generally the one who is willing to do and dare."
   — *Dale Carnegie*

"It does not matter how slowly you go (toward achieving your dream) so long as you do not stop."
   — *Confucius*

"Never discourage anyone who continually makes progress, no matter how slow."
   — *Plato*

"Slow and study wins the race."
   — *Unknown*

"Why do we grieve failures longer than we celebrate wins?"
   — *Komal Kapoor*

"If you run after two hares, you catch neither."
— *Unknown*

"The secret of getting ahead is getting started. The secret of getting started is breaking your complex overwhelming tasks into small manageable tasks, and starting on the first one."
— *Mark Twain*

"Be a maker in the morning and a manager in the afternoon."
— *Garry Keller*

"The only thing worse than starting something and failing… is not starting something."
— *Seth Godin*

"Our greatest glory is not in never failing, but in rising up every time we fail."
— *Ralph Waldo Emerson*

"It is impossible to live without failing at something, unless you live so cautiously that you might as well not have lived at all—in which case, you fail by default."
— *J.K. Rowling*

"The most difficult thing is the decision to act. The rest is merely tenacity."
— *Amelia Earhart*

"You can control two things; your work ethic and your attitude about anything."
— *Ali Krieger*

"You only have control over three things in your life. The thoughts you think, the images you visualize, and the action you take."
— *Jack Canfield*

"When something I can't control happens, I ask myself: Where is the hidden gift? Where is the positive in this?"

— *Sara Blakely*

"Create a definite plan for carrying out your desire and begin at once, whether you are ready or not, to put this plan into action."

— *Napoleon Hill*

> *"Starting before you are ready isn't easy, but if you want change—it's required."*
>
> — *Marie Forleo*

"Do the thing and you will have the power."

— *Ralph Waldo Emerson*

"I can do all things through him who strengthens me."

— *Philippians 4:13*

"Little by little becomes a lot."

— *Unknown*

"Half of getting there is having the confidence to show up—and keep showing up."

— *Sophia Amornso*

"Confidence in what you do is crucial, but that does not mean being delusional. You must always face the truth and then combat the obstacles as they appear."

— *Diane Von Furstenberg*

"Obstacles don't have to stop you. If you run into a wall, don't turn around and give up. Figure out how to climb it, go through it, or work around it."

— *Michael Jordan*

"If you don't have confidence, you'll always find a way not to win."

— *Carl Lewis*

"So we do not lose heart. Though our outer self is wasting away, our inner self is being renewed day by day. For this light momentary affliction is preparing for us an eternal weight of glory beyond all comparison, as we look not to the things that are seen but to the things that are unseen."
— *2 Corinthians 4: 16-18*

"To advance, stand fast under all circumstances."
— *B.C. Forbes*

"If you are going through hell, keep going."
— *Winston Churchill*

"Into each life some rain must fall."
— *Henry W. Longfellow*

"Perseverance is not a long race; it is many short races one after another."
— *Walter Elliot*

"Have faith in your journey. Everything had to happen exactly as it did to get where you are going next."
— *Mandy Hale*

"To get through the hardest journey we need to take only one step at a time, but we must keep on stepping."
— *Chinese Proverb*

"Work hard for what you want because it won't come to you without a fight. You have to be strong and courageous and know that you can do anything you put your mind to. If somebody puts you down or criticizes you, just keep on believing in yourself and turn it into something positive."
— *Leah LaBelle*

"Plans are great, but missions are better. Missions survive when plans fail, and plans almost always fail."
— *Seth Godin*

"A mission statement is not something you write overnight… But fundamentally, your mission statement becomes your constitution, the solid expression of your vision and values. It becomes the criterion by which you measure everything else in your life."
— *Stephen Covey*

"Develop success from failures. Discouragement and failure are two of the surest stepping stones to success."
— *Dale Carnegie*

"There is magic in endurance: It's allowing a stumbling block to become a stepping stone."
— *Reverend Run*

"What you share with the world is what it keeps of you."
— *Lisa Saputo*

"Exposure from a young age to the realities of the world is a super big thing."
— *Bill Gates*

"Patience attains all that it strives for."
— *St. Teresa of Avila*

"He that can have patience can have what he will."
— *Benjamin Franklin*

"When anyone can be persuaded to think spiritually, to have faith and believe, then the mind, being motivated to a higher level, open to maximum strength and amazing powers it possesses go to work on situations to bring about good results."
— *Dr. Norman Vincent Peale*

"Concentration is the secret of strength in politics, in war, in trade, in short in all management of human affairs."
— *Ralph Waldo Emerson*

"My motto is concentration. First honesty; then industry and then concentration."

— *Andrew Carnegie*

"In order to become rich, you must believe you can do it, and you must take the action necessary to achieve your goal."

— *Suze Orman*

"My advice is to focus on the importance of forging a long-term relationship, whether with colleagues, partners, or customers. It is often easy to get caught up in short-term decisions."

— *Sheila Lirio Marcelo*

"Don't let others convince you that the idea is good when your gut tells you it's bad."

— *Kevin Ross*

"Don't get distracted. Never tell yourself that you need to be the biggest brand in the whole world. Start by working on what you need at the present moment and then what you need to do tomorrow. So, set yourself manageable targets."

— *Jas Bagniewski*

"Today is life -- the only life you are sure of. Make the most of today. Get interested in something. Shake yourself awake. Develop a hobby. Let the winds of enthusiasm sweep through you. Live today with gusto."

— *Dale Carnegie*

"Do something today that your future self will thank you for."

— *Unknown*

"Stay focused on your goal rather than getting hung up on daily ups and downs."

— *Barack Obama*

"Stay true to yourself, yet always be open to learning. Work hard, and never give up on your dreams, even when nobody else believes they can come true but you. These are not cliches but real tools you need no matter what you do in life to stay focused on your path."
— *Phillip Sweet*

"Focus on being productive instead of busy."
— *Tim Ferriss*

"Winning means you're willing to go longer, work harder, and give more than anyone else."
— *Vince Lombardi*

"When you're riding, only the race in which you're riding is important."
— *Bill Shoemaker*

"We either make ourselves miserable, or we make ourselves strong. The amount of work is the same."
— *Carlos Castaneda*

"Everything that is not forbidden by laws of nature is achievable, given the right knowledge."
— *David Deutsch*

"All our knowledge has its origins in our perceptions."
— *Leonardo da Vinci*

"Science is nothing but perception."
— *Plato*

"Taking action is the only path to change."
— *Marie Forleo*

"An ounce of action is worth a ton of theory."
— *Ralph Waldo Emerson*

"We always overestimate the change that will occur in the next two years and underestimate the change that will occur in the next ten."
— *Bill Gates*

"No problem can withstand the assault of sustained thinking."
— *Voltaire*

"Thinking: the talking of the soul with itself."
— *Plato*

"A generous person will prosper; whoever refreshes others will be refreshed."
— *Proverbs 11:25*

"The rare individual who unselfishly tries to serve others has an enormous advantage."
— *Dale Carnegie*

"There are very few monsters who warrant the fear we have of them."
— *Andre Gide*

"The only thing we have to fear is fear itself."
— *Franklin D. Roosevelt*

"If a fear cannot be articulated, it can't be conquered."
— *Stephen King*

"The noblest pleasure is the joy of understanding."
— *Leonardo da Vinci*

"Understanding a question is half an answer."
— *Socrates*

"Life is a succession of lessons which must be lived to be understood."
— *Ralph Waldo Emerson*

"Seek first to understand, then to be understood."
— *Stephen Covey*

"Nothing in life is to be feared, it is only to be understood. Now is the time to understand more, so that we may fear less."
— *Marie Curie*

"I did not understand steam machinery, but I tried to understand much more complicated mechanism; – man."
— *Andrew Carnegie*

"You gain strength, courage, and confidence by every experience in which you really stop to look fear in the face."
— *Eleanor Roosevelt*

"Strength is a matter of the made-up mind."
— *John Beecher*

"People do not lack strength; they lack will."
— *Victor Hugo*

"Clarity comes from engagement, not from thought."
— *Marie Forleo*

"Everything is in the mind. That's where it all starts. Knowing what you want is the first step toward getting it."
— *Mae West*

"You don't need to see the whole staircase, just take the first step."
— *Martin Luther King, Jr.*

"Discovering what you really want saves you endless confusion and wasted energy."
— *Stuart Wilde*

"He who will not economize will have to agonize."
— *Confucius*

"Great achievement is usually born of great sacrifice, and never the result of selfishness."
— *Napoleon Hill*

"The secret of happiness is renunciation."
 — *Andrew Carnegie*

"Economy does not consist in saving the coal, but in using the time while it burns."
 — *Ralph Waldo Emerson*

"A decision delayed until it is too late is not a decision; it's an evasion."
 — *Unknown*

"It is never too late to be what you might have been."
 — *George Eliot*

"It's never too late for a new beginning in your life."
 — *Joyce Meyers*

"When in doubt, bootstrap. Using your own personal resources is the easiest way to start a business. You don't have to convince investors about the merits of your idea. You just have to convince yourself."
 — *Ryan Holmes*

"If you have a dream AND you have a job. That's amazing! You can learn how to navigate both. Your employer, or as I like to call it your 'investor', gives you the money to invest in your dream, and pay your bills while you chase your dreams."
 — *Lisa Nichols*

"Trust the instinct to no end, though you can render no reason."
 — *Ralph Waldo Emerson*

"It is better to suffer wrong than to do it, and happier to be sometimes cheated than not to trust."
 — *Samuel Johnson*

"Trust is the glue of life. It's the most essential ingredient in effective communication. It's the foundational principle that holds all relationships."
 — *Stephen Covey*

"Men love women who are courageous for it means they can go all the way with him in his pursuit of his good dreams and intentions."
>— *Agu Jaachynma N.E.*

"The most important thing that we entrepreneurs have is our human capital. If we exhaust it, we make bad decisions."
>— *Arianna Huffington*

"The best way to predict your future is to create it."
>— *Abraham Lincoln*

"The secret of your future is hidden in your daily routine."
>— *Mike Murdock*

"Always make your future bigger than your past."
>— *Dan Sullivan*

"When our memories outweigh our dreams, it is then that we become old."
>— *Bill Clinton*

"Patience is a virtue not a vice."
>— *Agu Jaachynma N.E.*

"Patience is bitter but its fruit is sweet."
>— *French Proverb*

"No matter what the industry you choose to ultimately invest all your time and energy in, be sure you're the owner, founder, and CEO. Remember, if you don't own it, you can't control it nor can you depend on it."
>— *Brandi L. Bates*

"The best investment is in the tools of one's own trade."
>— *Benjamin Franklin*

"It's not about getting out of your comfort zone to reach your goal. It's about widening your comfort zone so far that your goal fits comfortably inside. Once you do that, hitting your goals will be like hitting 3s for Steph Curry."
— *Richie Norton*

"Whatever goal you give to your subconscious mind, it will work night and day to achieve."
— *Jack Canfield*

"When it is obvious that the goals cannot be reached, don't adjust the goals, adjust the action steps."
— *Confucius*

"He that cannot reason is a fool. He that will not is a bigot. He that dare not is a slave."
— *Andrew Carnegie*

"You need to choose your association according to your vision."
— *Onyi Anyado*

"If you are working with no vision to be own your own boss, you are no different from people who are unemployed."
— *Sunday Adelaja*

"The most successful people in the world today are entrepreneurs."
— *Sunday Adelaja*

"Entrepreneurship is living a few years of your life like most people won't so you can spend the rest of your life like most people can't."
— *Unknown*

"Every successful person in the world is a hustler one way or another. We all hustle to get where we need to be. Only a fool would sit around and wait on another man to feed him.'
— *K'wan*

"But as an entrepreneur, you have to feel like you can jump out of an airplane because you're confident that you'll catch a bird flying by. It's an act of stupidity, and most entrepreneurs go splat because the bird doesn't come by, but a few times it does."
    — *Reed Hastings*

"What you seek is also seeking you."
    — *Rumi*

"The Lord loves the pure of heart; the man of winning speech has the king for his friend."
    — *Proverbs 22:11*

"Never regret a day in your life. Good days bring you happiness and bad days give you experience."
    — *Unknown*

"Whoever would love life and see good days must keep their tongue from evil and their lips from deceitful speech."
    — *1 Peter 3:10*

"To handle yourself, use your head; to handle others, use your heart."
    — *Eleanor Roosevelt*

"Apply your heart to instruction, and your ears to words of knowledge."
    — *Proverbs 23:12*

"For you will surely have a future, and your hope will not be cut off."
    — *Proverbs 23:18*

"Don't be afraid of waiting."
    — *Unknown*

"Stop being afraid of what could go wrong, and start being excited about what could go right."
    — *Anthony Robbins*

"Be strong and courageous. Do not be afraid or terrified because of them, for the LORD your God goes with you; he will never leave you nor forsake you."
— *Deuteronomy 31:6*

"Create your world with God's Word in your mouth. Just say it and it will be accomplished!"
— *Agu Jaachynma N.E.*

"Every act you have ever performed since the day you were born was because you wanted something. Aim for the highest and when it's a question of God's almighty spirit, never say I can't."
— *Andrew Carnegie*

"An entrepreneur tends to bite off a little more than he can chew hoping he'll quickly learn how to chew it."
— *Roy Ash*

"Getting out of your own way can be the hardest part about maintaining your drive and self-motivation. Some tasks require difficult solutions and hours of work, while others just seem impossible. When a task or problem seems insurmountable, the best thing to do is simply throw caution to the wind, set aside your fears or doubts, and simply act."
— *Unknown*

"You must take personal responsibility. You cannot change circumstances, the seasons, or the wind, but you can change yourself."
— *Jack Canfield*

"The key is taking responsibility and initiative, deciding what your life is about and prioritizing your life around the most important things."
— *Stephen Covey*

"A ship in the harbor is safe, but that is not what ships are built for."
— *John A. Shedd*

"If your dreams don't scare you, they are too small."
— *Sir. Richard Branson*

"If people are not laughing at your goals, your goals are too small."
— *Aziz Premji*

"If you don't have big dreams and goals, you'll end up working for someone that does."
— *Unknown*

"I have not failed. I've just found 10,000 ways that won't work."
— *Thomas A. Edison:*

"Someone is sitting in the shade today because someone planted a tree a long time ago."
— *Warren Buffett*

"What is life without a little risk."
— *J.K. Rowling*

"Don't risk more than you can afford to lose!"
— *Unknown*

"To a certain extent, a little blindness is necessary when you undertake a risk."
— *Bill Gates*

"Knowledge without action is meaningless"
— *Abu Bakr*

"Action is the real measure of intelligence."
— *Napoleon Hill*

"Never give up on a dream just because of the time it will take to accomplish it."
— *Earl Nightingale*

"Don't worry about being successful but work toward being significant and the success will naturally follow."
— *Oprah Winfrey*

"You need to spend all of your time and energy on creating something that actually brings value to the people you're asking for money."
— *Gary Vaynerchuk*

"What do you need to start a business? Three simple things: know your product better than anyone. Know your customer, and have a burning desire to succeed."
— *Dave Thomas*

"Success demands singleness of purpose."
— *Vince Lombardi*

"Starting a successful business is not tricky. Starting a successful business does not require above average intelligence. Starting a successful business does require having a pig-headed, purpose-driven tenacity about achieving your life goals and fulfilling your life's vision through providing products and services that offer uncompromising quality in a scalable and duplicatable way."
— *Clay Clark*

"You are the master of your destiny. You can influence, direct and control your own environment. You can make your life what you want it to be."
— *Napoleon Hill*

"Defeat is a state of mind; no one is ever defeated until defeat is accepted as a reality."
— *Bruce Lee*

"Sheer persistence is the difference between success and failure."
— *Donald Trump*

"Life has two rules: number 1, never quit! Number 2, always remember rule number one."
— *Duke Ellington*

"Win If You Can, Lose If You Must, But NEVER QUIT!"
— *Unknown*

"Life has many ways of testing a person's will, either by having nothing happen at all or by having everything happen all at once."
— *Paulo Coelho*

"Most people never run far enough on their first wind to find out they've got a second."
— *William James*

"Just keep going. Everybody gets better if they keep at it."
— *Ted Williams*

"The main thing is to keep the main thing the main thing."
— *Stephen Covey*

"Business is not just doing deals; business is having great products, doing great engineering and providing tremendous service to customers. Finally, business is a cobweb of human relationship."
— *Ross Perot*

"Your most unhappy customers are your greatest source of learning."
— *Bill Gates*

"Watch the costs and the profits will take care of themselves."
— *Andrew Carnegie*

"Do the hard jobs first. The easy jobs will take care of themselves."
— *Dale Carnegie*

"A business absolutely devoted to service will have one worry about profits. They will be embarrassingly large."
— *Henry Ford*

"The superior man understands what is right; the inferior man understands what will sell."
— *Confucius*

"Arouse in the other person an eager want. He who can do this has the whole world with him."
— *Dale Carnegie*

"No man can make you feel inferior without your consent."
— *Unknown*

"When you know your worth, no one can make you feel worthless."
— *Unknown*

"Extraordinary results become possible when where you want to go is completely aligned with what you do today."
— *Gary Keller*

"If you can tune into your purpose and really align with it, setting goals so that your vision is an expression of that purpose, then life flows much more easily."
— *Jack Canfield*

"One man with courage makes a majority."
— *Andrew Jackson*

"Act as if what you do makes a difference. It does."
— *William James*

"All men have fears, but the brave put down their fears and go forward."
— *Dale Carnegie*

"Don't dream about success. Get out there and work for it. You can cry, scream, and bang your head in frustration but keep pushing forward. It's worth it."
— *Unknown*

"Growth is never by mere chance; it is the result of forces working together."
— *James Cash Penney, (J.C. Penney)*

"The easiest, fastest, and best way to find out what is or isn't working is to pay attention to the results you are currently producing."
— *Jack Canfield*

"Falling down is how we grow. Staying down is how we die."
— *Brian Vaszily*

"Here is the simple but powerful rule… always give people more than they expect to get."
— *Nelson Boswell*

"My best advice to entrepreneurs is this: forget about making mistakes, just do it."
— *Ajaero Tony Martins*

"Our greatest glory is not in never falling, but in rising every time we fall."
— *Confucius*

"Don't try to beat the competitors at their game. You have to invent a new game---and master it."
— *Reid Hoffman*

"Men are not against you; they are merely for themselves."
— *Jon Christian Smuts*

"When you combine extreme focus and great teams, magic happens."
— *Sam Altman*

"One man can be a crucial ingredient on a team, but one man cannot make a team."
— *Kareem Abdul-Jabbar*

"No matter how brilliant your mind or strategy, if you're playing a solo game, you'll always lose out to a team."
— *Reid Hoffman*

"Teamwork is the ability to work together toward a common vision. It is the fuel that allows common people to attain uncommon results."
— *Andrew Carnegie*

"Talent wins games, but teamwork wins championships."
— *Michael Jordan*

"It is much more important to work on the right thing than it is to work many hours. Most people waste most of their time on stuff that doesn't matter."
— *Sam Altman*

"Things which matter most must never be at the mercy of things which matter least."
— *Johann Wolfgang Von Goethe*

"The things which are most important don't always scream the loudest."
— *Bob Hawke*

"Don't say you don't have enough time. You have exactly the same number of hours per day that were given to Helen Keller, Pasteur, Michelangelo, Mother Teresa, Leonardo Da Vinci, Thomas Jefferson, and Albert Einstein."
— *H. Jackson Brown, Jr.*

"The people who achieve extraordinary results don't achieve them by working more hours. They achieve them by getting more done in those hours they work."
— *Gary Keller*

"Once you have figured out what to do, be unstoppable about getting your small handful of priorities accomplished quickly. I have yet to meet a slow-moving person who is very successful."
— *Sam Altman*

"When you make a business, you get to make a little universe where you control all the laws."
— *Derek Sivers*

"Good men must not obey the laws too well."
— *Ralph Waldo Emerson*

"If you obey all the rules, you miss all the fun."
— *Katharine Hepburn*

"Reasons your product fail: Too complex. Can't easily be described. Didn't iterate fast enough. Bland. Failed to launch into a community. Doesn't save time/money. Poor design. Does too much. Didn't take a feature risk. Listened to the wrong customers."
— *Brian Norgard*

"In your actions, don't procrastinate. In your conversations, don't confuse. In your thoughts, don't wander. In your soul, don't be passive or aggressive. In your life, don't be all about business"
— *Marcus Aurelius*

"We must learn what customers really want, not what they say they want or what we think they want."
— *Eric Ries*

"Don't find customers for your products, find products for your customers."
— *Seth Godin*

"In a world where almost no one takes a truly long-term view, the market richly rewards those who do."
— *Sam Altman*

"No man becomes rich without himself enriching others."
— *Andrew Carnegie*

"The truth of things is the chief nutriment of superior intellects."
— *Leonardo da Vinci*

"No man, who continues to add something to the material, intellectual and moral well-being of the place in which he lives, is left long without proper reward."
   — *Booker T. Washington*

"A business that makes nothing but money is a poor business."
   — *Henry Ford*

"After a certain point, money is meaningless. It ceases to be the goal. The game is what counts."
   — *Aristotle Onassis*

"The life of money-making is one undertaken under compulsion, and wealth is evidently not the good we are seeking; for it is merely useful and for the sake of something else."
   — *Aristotle*

"There is no class as pitiably wretched as that which possesses money and nothing else."
   — *Andrew Carnegie*

"I learned to go into business only with people whom I like, trust, and admire."
   — *Warren Buffett*

"Deliberately seek the company of people who influence you to think and act on building the life you desire."
   — *Napoleon Hill*

"Success in dealing with people depends on a sympathetic grasp of the other person's viewpoint."
   — *Dale Carnegie*

"When you work on something, if you fall in love with it, that's a good sign. If you do, others will."
   — *Elon Musk*

"You have to be burning with an idea, or a problem, or a wrong that you want to right. If you're not passionate enough from the start, you'll never stick it out."
— *Steve Job*

"People rarely succeed unless they have fun in what they are doing."
— *Dale Carnegie*

"Big results require big ambitions."
— *Heraclitus*

"Without ambition one starts nothing. Without work one finishes nothing. The prize will not be sent to you. You have to win it."
— *Ralph Waldo Emerson*

"For you to achieve extraordinary results, the people surrounding you and your physical surrounding must support your goals."
— *Garry Keller*

"My parents were just constantly affirming me in everything that I did. Late at night, I'd wake up and hear my mother talking over my bed, saying, 'You're going to do great on this test. You can do anything you want.'"
— *Stephen Covey*

"It's okay to outgrow people who don't grow. Grow tall always."
— *Unknown*

"Take criticism seriously, but not personally. If there is truth or merit in the criticism, try to learn from it. Otherwise, let it roll right off you."
— *Hillary Clinton*

"Work hard and don't give up hope. Be open to criticism and keep learning. Surround yourself with happy, warm and genuine people."
— *Tena Desae*

"The world is full of nice people. If you can't find one, be one."
— *Nishan Panwar*

"Three-fourths of the people you will meet are hungering for sympathy. Give it to them and they will love you."
— *Dale Carnegie*

"Easy paths, crowded destinations."
— *Scott Belsky*

"Do one thing every day that scares you."
— *Eleanor Roosevelt*

"Every time you take a risk or move out of your comfort zone, you have a great opportunity to learn more about yourself and your capacity."
— *Jack Canfield*

"I always did something I was a little not ready to do. I think that's how you grow. When there's that moment of Wow, I'm not really sure I can do this, and you push through those moment, that's when you have a breakthrough."
— *Marissa Mayer*

"If we wait until we're ready, we'll be waiting for the rest of our lives."
— *Lemony Snicket*

"If it scares you, it might be a good thing to try."
— *Seth Godin*

"When I let go of what I am, I become what I might be."
— *Lao-Tzu*

"Prioritizing is the most important thing in business."
— *Noah Kagan*

"The key is not to prioritize what's on your schedule, but to schedule your priorities.
— *Stephen Covey*

"It's not about ideas. It's about making ideas happen."
— *Scott Belsky*

"No matter what people tell you, words and ideas can change the world."
— *Robin Williams*

"If you don't ask, the answer is always no."
— *Nora Roberts*

"People who ask confidently get more than those who are hesitant and uncertain. When you've figured out what you want to ask for, do it with certainty, boldness and confidence."
— *Jack Canfield*

"Everyone knows that you need a great team, great execution, and a great idea. Less obvious is that you have to have great endurance."
— *Sam Altman*

"You will either step forward into growth or you will step back into safety."
— *Abraham Maslow*

"Chase the vision, not the money. The money will end up following you."
— *Tony Hsieh*

"The bravest are surely those who have the clearest vision of what is before them, glory and danger alike, and yet notwithstanding, go out to meet it."
— *Thucydides*

"If you wake up deciding what you want to give versus what you're going to get, you become a more successful person. In other words, if you want to make money, you have to help someone else make money."
— *Russell Simmons*

"Dwell on the beauty of life. Watch the stars, and see yourself running with them."

— *Marcus Aurelius*

"The adventure of life is to learn. The purpose of life is to grow. The nature of life is to change. The challenge of life is to overcome. The essence of life is to care. The opportunity of life is to serve. The secret of life is to dare. The spice of life is to befriend. The beauty of life is to give."

— *William Arthur Ward*

"If you don't have a competitive advantage, don't compete."

— *Jack Welch*

"And the law of competition may be sometimes hard for the individual but it's best for the race because it ensures the survival of the fittest in every department."

— *Andrew Carnegie*

"Don't compare yourself with anyone in this world. If you do so, you are insulting yourself."

— *Bill Gates*

"Don't compare yourself to others. Be like the sun and the moon and shine when it's your time."

— *Unknown*

"I generally find that comparison is the fast track to unhappiness."

— *Jack Canfield*

"Your playing small does not serve the world. There is nothing enlightened about shrinking so that other people won't feel insecure around you. We are all meant to shine, as children do."

— *Marianne Williamson*

"The only way I can get you to do anything is by giving you what you want."

— *Dale Carnegie*

"When you are content to be simply yourself and don't compare to compete, everybody will respect you."
— *Lao-Tzu*

"You become whatever metric you choose to measure yourself by."
— *Brian Norgard*

"Products that work in a big group first worked in a tiny group. Small town before big city. A thriving local population leads to a booming global trend."
— *Brian Norgard*

"It is better to act too quickly than it is to wait too long."
— *Jack Welch*

"When you do not know what to do---wait."
— *Unknown*

"Creating space to think is a competitive advantage."
— *Greg McKeown*

"Originality is simply a pair of fresh eyes."
— *Thomas W. Higginson*

"There are two types of people who will tell you that you cannot make a difference in the world: those who are afraid to try and those who are afraid you will succeed."
— *Ray Goforth*

"You don't know what you can miss before you try."
— *Franklin Pierce*

"When you stop chasing the wrong things, you give the right things a chance to catch you."
— *Lolly Daskal*

"Stop chasing the money and start chasing the passion."
— *Tony Hsieh*

"Yesterday I was clever, so I wanted to change the world. Today I am wise, so I am changing myself."
— *Rumi*

"The ones who are crazy enough to think they can change the world, are the ones that do."
— *Unknown*

"If you are not willing to risk the usual, you will have to settle for the ordinary."
— *Jim Rohn*

"All progress takes place outside the comfort zone."
— *Michael John Bobak*

"If you're walking down the right path and you're willing to keep walking, eventually you'll make progress."
— *Barack Obama*

"If you really look closely, most overnight successes took a long time."
— *Steve Jobs*

"Everything valuable takes time; there are no overnight successes."
— *Jack Canfield*

"I built a conglomerate and emerged the richest black man in the world in 2008 but it didn't happen overnight. It took me 30 years to get to where I am today. Youths of today aspire to be like me but they want to achieve it overnight. It's not going to work. To build a successful business, you must start small and dream big. In the journey of entrepreneurship, tenacity of purpose is supreme."
— *Aliko Dangote*

"Don't let the fear of losing be greater than the excitement of winning."
— *Robert Kiyosaki*

"The more difficult the victory, the greater the happiness in winning."
— *Pele*

"Winning is great, sure, but if you are really going to do something in life, the secret is learning how to lose. Nobody goes undefeated all the time. If you can pick up after a crushing defeat, and go on to win again, you are going to be a champion someday."

— *Wilma Rudolph*

"Champions keep playing until they get it right."

— *Billy Jean King*

"Everyone faces defeat. It may be a stepping-stone or a stumbling block, depending on the mental attitude with which it is faced."

— *Napoleon Hill*

"I've learned that something constructive comes from every defeat."

— *Tom Landry*

"The only limit to our realization of tomorrow will be our doubts of today."

— *Franklin D. Roosevelt*

"Doubt whom you will, but never yourself."

— *Christian Nestell Bovee*

"Unsuccessful people make their decisions based on their current situations. Successful people make their decision based on where they want to be."

— *Benjamin Hardy*

"Successful people are not gifted; they just work hard, then succeed on purpose."

— *G.K. Nielson*

"Life is like riding a bicycle. To keep your balance, you must keep moving."

— *Albert Einstein*

"Success seems to be connected with action. Successful people keep moving. They make mistakes, but they don't quit."
    — Conrad Hilton

"Don't watch the clock, do what it does. Keep going."
    — Sam Levenson

"If you can't make a mistake, you can't make anything."
    — Marva Collin

"The proactive approach to a mistake is to acknowledge it instantly, correct and learn from it."
    — Stephen Covey

"Don't quit yet, the worst moments are usually followed by the most beautiful silver linings. You have to stay strong, remember to keep your head up and remain hopeful."
    — Unknown

"I hated every minute of training, but I said, Don't quit. Suffer now and live the rest of your life a champion."
    — Muhammad Ali

"If you really want to do something, you'll find a way. If you don't you'll find an excuse."
    — Jim Rohn

"I attribute my success to this: I never gave or took an excuse."
    — Florence Nightingale

"Success is not the key to happiness. Happiness is the key to success. If you love what you are doing, you will be successful."
    — Albert Schweitzer

"Success is no accident. It is hard work, perseverance, learning, studying, sacrifice and most of all, love of what you are doing or learning to do."
    — Pele

"Success is good at any age, but the sooner you find it, the longer you will enjoy it."

— *Napoleon Hill*

"What you do today can improve all your tomorrows."

— *Ralph Marston*

"Leave nothing for tomorrow which can be done today."

— *Abraham Lincoln*

"As a well-spent day brings happy sleep, so a life well spent brings happy death."

— *Leonardo da Vinci*

"You are today where your thoughts have brought you; you will be tomorrow where your thoughts take you."

— *James Allen*

"The revelation of thought takes men out of servitude and into freedom."

— *Ralph Waldo Emerson*

"Opportunities don't happen. You create them."

— *Chris Grosser*

"I had to make my own living and my own opportunity. But I made it! Don't sit down and wait for the opportunities to come. Get up and make them."

— *Madam C.J. Walker*

"There is no scarcity of opportunity to make a living at what you love; there's only scarcity of resolve to make it happen."

— *Wayne Dyer*

"If you can dream it, you can do it."

— *Walt Disney*

"The difference between who you are and who you want to be is what you do."

— *Unknown*

"Success isn't about how much money you make; it's about the difference you make in people's lives."

— *Michelle Obama*

"In order to succeed, we must first believe that we can."

— *Nikos Kazantzakis*

"Doing well is the result of doing good. That's what capitalism is all about."

— *Ralph Waldo Emerson*

"Don't be distracted by criticism. Remember—the only taste of success some people get is to take a bit out of you."

— *Zig Ziglar*

"Criticism is dangerous because it wounds a person's pride, hurts his sense of importance, and arouses resentment."

— *Dale Carnegie*

"The secret of success is to do the common thing uncommonly well."

— *John D. Rockefeller, Jr.*

"You know you are on the road to success if you would do your job, and not be paid for it."

— *Oprah Winfrey*

"The man who does more than he is paid for will soon be paid for more than he does."

— *Napoleon Hill*

"There is a powerful driving force inside every human being that, once unleashed, can make any vision, dream, or desire a reality."

— *Anthony Robbins*

"I call myself a peaceful warrior because the battles we fight are on the inside."
— *Socrates*

"The secret to success is to know something nobody else knows."
— *Aristotle Onassis*

"The only place where success comes before work is in the dictionary."
— *Vidal Sassoon*

"Success comes to those who become success conscious."
— *Napoleon Hill*

"When you put together deep knowledge about a subject that intensely matters to you, charisma happens. You gain courage to share your passion, and when you do that, folks follow."
— *Jerry Porras*

"One of the huge mistakes people make is that they try to force an interest on themselves. You don't choose your passions; your passions choose you."
— *Jeff Bezos*

"Passion is energy. Feel the power that comes from focusing on what excites you."
— *Oprah Winfrey*

"Make the best use of what's in your power and take the rest as it happens."
— *Epictetus*

"Never ever chase money. You should chase success, because with success money follows."
— *Wilfred Emmanuel-Jones*

"Logic will get you from A to B. Imagination will take you everywhere."
— *Albert Einstein*

"The will to win, the desire to succeed, the urge to reach your full potential...these are the keys that will unlock the door to personal excellence."
— *Confucius*

"Everyone has inside them a piece of good news. The good news is you don't know how great you can be! How much you can love! What you can accomplish! And what your potential is."
— *Anne Frank*

"Excellence is the gradual result of always striving to do better."
— *Pat Riley*

"If at first you don't succeed, you are running about average."
— *M.H. Alderson*

"To win without risk is to triumph without glory."
— *Corneille*

"Keep away from people who try to belittle your ambitions. Small people always do that, but the really great make you feel that you, too, can become great."
— *Mark Twain*

"The very substance of the ambitious is merely the shadow of a dream."
— *William Shakespeare*

"There is only one success- to be able to spend your life in your own way."
— *Christopher Morley*

"Whatever the mind can conceive and believe, the mind can achieve."
— *Napoleon Hill*

"The mind is the limit. As long as the mind can envision the fact that you can do something, you can do it, as long as you really believe 100 percent."
— *Arnold Schwarzenegger*

"What is not started will never get finished."
— *Johann Wolfgang von Goethe*

"When you cease to dream you cease to live."
— *Malcolm Forbes*

"Education is the most powerful weapon which you can use to change the world."
— *Nelson Mandela*

"If a man neglects his education, he walks lame to the end of his life."
— *Plato*

"Formal education will make you a living; self-education will make you a fortune."
— *Jim Rohn*

"If you want your child to get the best education possible, it is actually more important to get him assigned to a great teacher than to a great school."
— *Bill Gates*

"When it comes to developing character strength, inner security and unique personal and interpersonal talents and skills in a child, no institution can or ever will compare with, or effectively substitute for, the home's potential for positive influence."
— *Stephen Covey*

"The most important part of education is proper training in the nursery."
— *Plato*

"You are not here merely to make a living. You are here in order to enable the world to live more amply, with greater vision, with a finer spirit of hope and achievement. You are here to enrich the world, and you impoverish yourself if you forget the errand."
— *Woodrow Wilson*

"Be not afraid of greatness: some are born great, some achieve greatness, and some have greatness thrust upon them."
— *William Shakespeare*

"Never underestimate the power of dreams and the influence of the human spirit. We are all the same in this notion: The potential for greatness lives within each of us."
— *Wilma Rudolph*

"In the midst of chaos, there is also opportunity."
— *Sun-Tzu*

"When you strive for greatness, chaos is guaranteed to show up."
— *Gary Keller*

"The most valuable thing you can make is a mistake- you can't learn anything from being perfect."
— *Adam Osborne*

"If everything was perfect, you would never learn and you would never grow."
— *Beyonce Knowles*

"Better a little which is well done, than a great deal imperfectly."
— *Plato*

"You don't have to be perfect to be amazing."
— *Unknown*

"Unless you try to do something beyond what you have already mastered, you will never grow."
— *Ralph Waldo Emerson*

"A leader is one who knows the way, goes the way, and shows the way."
— *John C. Maxwell*

"The function of leadership is to produce more leaders, not more followers."
— *Ralph Nader*

"A good leader can let you fail and yet not let you be a failure."
— *Stanley McChrystal*

"People buy into the leader before they buy into the vision."
— *John C. Maxwell."*

"Leaders think and talk about the solutions. Followers think and talk about the problem."
— *Brian Tracy*

"If you look to lead, invest at least 40% of your time managing yourself – your ethics, character, principles, purpose, motivation, and conduct. Invest at least 30% managing those with authority over you, and 15% managing your peers."
— *Dee Hock*

"Aspiring entrepreneurs have to actually do something that they feel strongly passionate about, and in most cases, they should seek inspiration from their own experience… If you had a terrible experience, you should despise the experience to the extent that you are continuously seeking a solution for it."
— *Best Ayiorwoth*

"We lost because we told ourselves we lost."
— *Count Leo Tolstoy*

"Superior leaders are willing to admit a mistake and cut their losses. Be willing to admit that you've changed your mind. Don't persist when the original decision turns out to be a poor one."
— *Brian Tracy*

"No person will make a great leader who wants to do it all himself or get all the credit for doing it."
— *Andrew Carnegie*

"It is not strange… to mistake change for progress"
— *Millard Fillmore*

"Choose a job that you like, and you will never have to work a day in your life."
— *Confucius*

"Don't judge each day by the harvest you reap but by the seeds that you plant."
— *Robert Louis Stevenson*

"Make each day your masterpiece."
— *John Wooden*

"Every time you state what you want or believe, you're the first to hear it. It's a message to both you and others about what you think is possible. Don't put a ceiling on yourself."
— *Oprah Winfrey*

"Your work is going to fill a large part of your life, and the only way to be truly satisfied is to do what you believe is great work. And the only way to do great work is to love what you do."
— *Steve Jobs*

"If it ain't fun, don't do it."
— *Jack Canfield*

"For all sad words of tongue or pen, the saddest are these: "It might have been!"
— *John Greenleaf Whittier*

"I knew that if I failed I wouldn't regret that, but I knew the one thing I might regret is not trying."
— *Jeff Bezos*

"You'll seldom experience regret for anything that you've done. It is what you haven't done that will torment you. The message, therefore, is clear. Do it! Develop an appreciation for the present moment. Seize every second of your life and savor it."
— *Wayne Dyer*

"The fault, dear Brutus, is not in our stars, but in ourselves, that we are underlings."
— *William Shakespeare*

"Don't limit yourself. Many people limit themselves to what they think they can do. You can go as far as your mind lets you. What you believe, remember, you can achieve."
— *Mary Kay Ash*

"Only those who will risk going too far can possible find out how far one can go."
— *T.S. Eliot*

"When you find an idea that you just can't stop thinking about, that's probably a good one to pursue."
— *Josh James*

"Think big. Start small"
— *Seth Godin*

"The fastest way to change yourself is to hang out with people who are already the way you want to be."
— *Reid Hoffman*

"In the end, a vision without the ability to execute it is probably a hallucination."
— *Steve Case*

"Vision is the art of seeing things invisible."
— *Jonathan Swift*

"Only he who can see the invisible can do the impossible."
— *Frank. Gaines*

"Risk more than others think is safe. Dream more than others think is practical."
— *Howard Schultz*

"The man who acquires the ability to take full possession of his own mind may take possession of anything else to which he is justly entitled."
— *Andrew Carnegie*

"The way to get started is to quit talking and begin doing."
— *Walt Disney*

"I have been impressed with the urgency of doing. Knowing is not enough; we must apply. Being willing is not enough; we must do."
— *Leonardo da Vinci*

"Words without actions are the assassins of idealism."
— *Herbert Hoover*

"When you have talked yourself into what you want, right there is the place to stop talking and begin saying it with deeds."
— *Napoleon Hill*

"Be happy with what you have while working for what you want."
— *Helen Keller*

"Be great in act, as you have been in thought"
— *William Shakespeare*

"There are lots of bad reasons to start a company. But there's only one good, legitimate reason, and I think you know what it is: it's to change the world."
— *Phil Libin*

"The important thing is not being afraid to take a chance. Remember, the greatest failure is to not try. Once you find something you love to do, be the best at doing it."

— *Debbi Fields*

"You shouldn't focus on why you can't do something, which is what most people do. You should focus on why perhaps you can, and be one of the exceptions."

— *Steve Case*

"Empower yourself and realize the importance of contributing to the world by living your talent. Work on what you love. You are responsible for the talent that has been entrusted to you."

— *Catharina Bruns*

"I'm convinced that about half of what separates the successful entrepreneurs from the non-successful ones is pure perseverance."

— *Steve Jobs*

"It is always the start that requires the greatest effort."

— *James Cash Penney, (J.C. Penney)*

"Despite the struggle, the pain, and the enormous sacrifice being an entrepreneur takes… it's worth it"

— *Joe Polish*

"The struggle you're in today is developing the strength you need tomorrow."

— *Robert Tew*

"The LORD is my light and my salvation; whom shall I fear? The LORD is the stronghold of my life; of whom shall I be afraid?"

— *Psalm 27:12*

"Strength does not come from physical capacity. It comes from an indomitable will."

— *Mahatma Gandhi*

"Strength does not come from winning. Your struggles develop your strength. When you go through hardships and decide not to surrender, that is strength."

— *Arnold Schwarzenegger*

"Every day may not be good…but there's something good in every day."

— *Alice Morse Earle*

"Happiness is the only things that multiplies when you share it."

— *Albert Schweitzer*

"The happiness of your life depends upon the quality of your thoughts."

— *Marcus Aurelius*

"The good life is a process, not a state of being. It is a direction, not a destination."

— *Carl Rogers*

"A truly happy person is one who can enjoy the scenery while on a detour."

— *Unknown*

"If you love your work, if you enjoy it, you're already a success."

— *Jack Canfield*

"Build something 100 people love, not something 1 million people kind of like."

— *Brian Chesky*

"We didn't set out to build a product. We set out to solve a problem."

— *Naval Ravikant*

"A company becomes the people it hires, not the plan it makes."

— *Sam Altman*

"The first requisite in running a major corporation is the ability to pick good people."
— *Lee Iacocca*

"Almost everyone underestimates the value of fast movers, in almost every context. Work with them. Be one yourself."
— *Sam Altman*

"The best time to plant a tree was 20 years ago. The second best time is now."
— *Chinese proverb*

"If people are doubting how far you can go, go so far that you can't hear them anymore."
— *Michele Ruiz*

"I didn't get there by wishing for it or hoping for it, but by working for it."
— *Estée Lauder*

"Success is falling nine times and getting up ten."
— *Jon Bon Jovi*

"Don't stop when you are tired. Stop when you are done."
— *Unknown*

"If you want a million dollar a year business, you can't do it with $50,000 a year capability."
— *Joe Polish*

"It always seems impossible until it is done."
— *Nelson Mandela*

"You always pass failure on the way to success."
— *Mickey Rooney*

"On the formula to build a billion-dollar Internet company: Take a human desire, preferably one that has been around for a really long time… identify that desire and use modern technology to take out steps."

— *Ev Williams*

"There are only three measurements that tell you nearly everything you need to know about your organization's overall performance: employee engagement, customer satisfaction, and cash flow."

— *Jack Welch*

"The quickest way to ruin the productivity of a small company is to have it adopt the practices of a large company."

— *David Heinemeir Hansson*

"Great things are done by a series of small things brought together."

— *Vincent Van Gogh*

"Great things in business are never done by one person, they're done by a team of people."

— *Steve Jobs*

"A day of sorrow is longer than a month of joy."

— *Chinese proverb*

"No possession is joyous without a companion."

— *St. Thomas Aquina*

"I find it wholesome to be alone the greater part of the time. To be in company, even with the best, is soon wearisome and dissipating. I love to be alone. I never found the companion that was so companionable as solitude."

— *William David Thoreau*

"Associate yourself with people of good quality, for it is better to be alone than in bad company"

— *Booker T. Washington*

"Pay every debt as if God wrote the bill."
— *Ralph Waldo Emerson*

"A wise person knows many things, but a successful person knows many people. We can't do it alone. Other people can change our lives and take us a lot further than we ever thought we could go."
— *Queen Latifh*

"He that walketh with wise men shall be wise."
Proverbs 13:20

"The art of being wise is the art of knowing what to overlook."
— *William James*

"Most big transformations come about from the hundreds of tiny, almost imperceptible, steps we take along the way."
— *Lori Gottlieb*

"Give a good idea to a mediocre team, and they will screw it up. But give a mediocre idea to a good team, and they will either fix it or come up with something better."
— *Ed Catmull*

"If it's a good idea, go ahead and do it. It's much easier to apologize than it is to get permission."
— *Grace Hopper*

"Don't be pushed around by the fears in your mind. Be led by the dreams in your heart."
— *Roy T. Bennett*

"The only place where your dreams become impossible is in your own thinking."
— *Robert H. Shuller*

"This is a reminder to you to create your own rule book, and live your life the way you want it."
— *Reese Evans*

"Impossible is just a big word thrown around by small men who find it easier to live in the world they've been given than to explore the power they have to change it. Impossible is not a fact. It's an opinion. Impossible is not a declaration. It's a dare. Impossible is potential. Impossible is temporary. Impossible is nothing."
— *Muhammad Ali*

"Opinion is the medium between knowledge and ignorance."
— *Plato*

"What is the difference between an obstacle and an opportunity? Our attitude towards it. Every opportunity has a difficult, and every difficulty has an opportunity."
— *J. Sidlow Baxter*

"In the middle of difficulty lies opportunity."
— *Albert Einstein*

"A negative mind will never give you a positive life."
— *Unknown*

"An attitude of positive expectation is the mark of the superior personality."
— *Brian Tracy*

"I'm not in this world to live up to your expectations and you're not in this world to live up to mine."
— *Bruce Lee*

"The positive thinker sees the invisible, feels the intangible, and achieves the impossible."
— *Winston Churchill*

"Continuous improvement is better than delayed perfection."
— *Mark Twain*

"Have the end in mind and every day make sure you're working towards it."

— *Ryan Allis*

"Begin with the end in mind. Start with the end outcome and work backwards to make your dream possible."

— *Wayne Dyer*

"It's not what you do once in a while it's what you do day in and day out that makes the difference."

— *Jenny Craig*

"Don't worry about failure; you only have to be right once."

— *Drew Houston*

"Continuous learning is the minimum requirement for success in any field."

— *Dennis Waitle*

"The learning and knowledge that we have, is, at the most, but little compared with that of which we are ignorant."

— *Plato*

"I believe in this concept that you learn by teaching."

— *Stephen Covey*

"Never stop learning because life never stops teaching."

— *Unknown*

"Study successful people and businesses, then do what they did to become successful while making slight modifications to fit your life style, your values, your business model and your goals."

— *Clay Clark*

"The best entrepreneurs are obsessed about one thing."

— *Maxime Lagacé*

"Pick an industry where you can play long term games with long term people."

— *Naval Ravikant*

"Build something you yourself want" is to startups what "Write what you know" to writing"

— *Paul Graham*

"Things are as seldom and bleak as they seem when they are going wrong—or as good as they seem when they are going well."

— *Dave Kekich*

"I never did anything worth doing by accident, nor did any of my inventions come indirectly through accident, except the phonograph. No, when I have fully decided that a result is worth getting, I go about it, and make trial after trial, until it comes."

— *Thomas A. Edison*

"I am not a product of my circumstances. I am a product of my decisions."

— *Stephen Covey*

"The percentage of mistakes in quick decisions is no greater than in long, drawn-out vacillations, and the effect of decisiveness itself "makes things go" and create confidence."

— *Anne O'Hare McCormick*

"The price of success is hard work, dedication to the job at hand, and the determination that whether we win or lose, we have applied the best of ourselves to the task at hand."

— *Vince Lombardi*

"You've got to get up every morning with determination if you're going to go to bed with satisfaction."

— *George Lorimer*

"If hard work is the key to success, most people would rather pick the lock."
— *Claude McDonald*

"The critical ingredient is getting off your butt and doing something. It's as simple as that. A lot of people have ideas, but there are few who decide to do something about them now. Not tomorrow. Not next week. But today. The true entrepreneur is a doer, not a dreamer."
— *Nolan Bushnell*

"I've learned that mistakes can often be as good a teacher as success."
— *Jack Welch*

"Smart people learn from everything and everyone. Average people from their experiences. Stupid people already have all the answers."
— *Socrates*

"Success is a lousy teacher. It seduces smart people into thinking they can't lose."
— *Bill Gates*

"It raises one above the herd and gives one a feeling of nobility and exaltation to admit one's mistakes."
— *Dale Carnegie*

"Show me a person who never made a mistake, and I will show you a person who never did anything."
— *William Rosenberg*

"Success is getting what you want. Happiness is wanting what you get."
— *Dale Carnegie*

"Most great people have attained their greatest success just one step beyond their greatest failure."
— *Napoleon Hill*

"If you are clear about your goals and take several steps in the right direction every day, eventually you will succeed. So decide what it is you want, write it down, review it constantly, and each day do something that moves you toward those goals."
— *Jack Canfield*

"If what you are doing is not moving you towards your goals, then it's moving you away from your goals."
— *Brian Tracy*

"Make your team feel respected, empowered and genuinely excited about the company's mission."
— *Tim Westergen*

"An empowered organization is one in which individuals have the knowledge, skill, desire, and opportunity to personally succeed in a way that leads to collective organizational success."
— *Stephen Covey*

"If you just work on stuff that you like and you're passionate about, you don't have to have a master plan with how things will play out."
— *Mark Zuckerberg*

"Anything you build on a large scale or with intense passion invites chaos."
— *Francis Ford Coppola*

"You can't ask customers what they want and then try to give that to them. — the time you get it built, they'll want something new."
— *Steve Jobs*

"Get big quietly, so you don't tip off potential competitors."
— *Chris Dixon*

"Don't play games that you don't understand, even if you see lots of other people making money from them."
— *Tony Hsieh*

"If you don't find a way to make money while you sleep, you will work until you die."

— *Warren Buffett*

"The difference between a boss and a leader: a boss says 'Go!' – a leader says, 'Let's go!'."

— *E.M Kelly*

"Always deliver more than expected."

— *Larry Page*

"You just have to pay attention to what people need and what has not been done."

— *Russell Simmons*

"Hire character. Train skill."

— *Peter Schultz*

"If you hire people just because they can do a job, they'll work for your money. But if you hire people who believe what you believe, they'll work for you with blood and sweat and tears."

— *Simon Sinek*

"Judge your natural character by what you do in your dreams."

— *Ralph Waldo Emerson*

"It's almost always harder to raise capital than you thought it would be, and it always takes longer. So plan for that."

— *Richard Harroch*

"If you approach 100 people for seed capital, 99 of them may say no, you just need that one."

— *Dr. William Pickard*

"The things we fear the most in organizations- fluctuations, disturbances, imbalances – are the primary sources of creativity."

— *Margaret Wheatley*

"Effective communication is 20% what you know and 80% how you feel about what you know."
— *Jim Rohn*

"The surest way to establish your credit is to work yourself into the position of not needing any."
— *Maurice Switzer*

"Stay self-funded as long as possible."
— *Garrett Camp*

"It's more effective to do something valuable than to hope a logo or name will say it for you."
— *Jason Cohen*

"Efficiency is doing the thing right. Effectiveness is doing the right thing."
— *Peter Drucker*

"Relentlessly strive to come up with new and better products and produce them more efficiently than the alternatives."
— *Charles G. Koch*

"The key responsibility of leadership is to think about the future. No one else can do it for you."
— *Brian Tracy*

"Effective leadership is putting first things first. Effective management is discipline, carrying it out."
— *Stephen Covey*

"Responsibilities gravitate to the person who can shoulder them."
— *Elbert Hubbard*

"It's not the load that breaks you down, it's the way you carry it."
— *Lena Horne*

"Don't worry about funding if you don't need it. Today it's cheaper to start a business than ever."

— *Noah Everett*

"Data beats emotions."

— *Sean Rad*

"Be undeniably good. No marketing effort or social media buzzword can be a substitute for that."

— *Anthony Volodkin*

"Make your product easier to buy than your competition, or you will find your customers buying from them, not you."

— *Mark Cuban*

"Openly share and talk to people about your idea. Use their lack of interest or doubt to fuel your motivation to make it happen."

— *Todd Garland*

"People who are unable to motivate themselves must be content with mediocrity, no matter how impressive their other talents."

— *Andrew Carnegie*

"You can motivate by fear, and you can motivate by reward. But both those methods are only temporary. The only lasting thing is self-motivation."

— *Homer Rice*

"Motivation comes from working on things we care about."

— *Sheryl Sandberg*

"I believe in destiny. But I also believe that you can't just sit back and let destiny happen. A lot of times, an opportunity might fall into your lap, but you have to be ready for that opportunity. You can't sit there waiting on it. A lot of times you are going to have to get out there and make it happen."

— *Spike Lee*

"No one is ready for a thing until he believes he can acquire it."
— *Napoleon Hill*

"If you are working on something that you really care about, you don't have to be pushed. The vision pulls you."
— *Steve Jobs*

"Failure will never overtake me if my determination to succeed is strong enough."
— *Og Mandino*

"The difference between the impossible and the possible lies in a person's determination."
— *Tommy Lasorda*

"Taking the first step is the difference between actually pursuing your passion and just dreaming about it."
— *Jack Canfield*

"Entrepreneurs are great at dealing with uncertainty and also very good at minimizing risk. That's the classic entrepreneur."
— *Mohnish Pabrai*

"We may encounter many defeats but we must not be defeated."
— *Maya Angelou*

"When defeat comes, accept it as a signal that your plans are not sound, rebuild those plans, and set sail once more toward your coveted goal."
— *Napoleon Hill*

"Knowing is not enough, we must apply. Wishing is not enough; we must do."
— *Johann Wolfgang Von Goethe*

"Imagine your life is perfect in every respect; What would it look like?"
— *Brian Tracy*

"If there is a book that you want to read, but it hasn't been written yet, you must be the one to write it."

— *Toni Morrison*

"We generate fears while we sit. We overcome them by action."

— *Dr. Henry Link*

"Security is mostly a superstition. Life is either a daring adventure or nothing."

— *Helen Keller*

"The man who has confidence in himself gains the confidence of others."

— *Hasidic Proverb*

"It's hard to lead a cavalry charge if you think you look funny on a horse."

— *Adlai E. Stevenson II*

"Creativity is intelligence having fun."

— *Albert Einstein*

"Do what you can with all you have, where you are."

— *Theodore Roosevelt*

"There are no limits to what you can accomplish, except the limits you place on your own thinking."

— *Brian Tracy*

"You have brains in your head. You have feet in your shoes. You can steer yourself any direction you choose. You're on your own. And you know what you know. And YOU are the one who'll decide where to go."

— *Dr. Seuss*

"Think as big as you possibly can and base what you do, how you do it, and who you do it with on succeeding at that level."

— *Gar Keller*

"Develop an attitude of gratitude. Say thank you to everyone you meet for everything they do for you."

— *Brain Tracy*

"Gratitude is not only the greatest of virtues, but the parent of all others."

— *Cicero*

"Gratitude is the single most important ingredient to living a successful and fulfilled life."

— *Jack Canfield*

"You are never too old to set another goal or to dream a new dream."

— *C.S. Lewis*

"To see what is right and not do it is a lack of courage."

— *Confucius*

"Wisdom equals knowledge plus courage. You have to not only know what to do and when to do it, but you have to also be brave enough to follow through."

— *Jarod Kintz*

"Wisdom is always an overmatch for strength."

— *Phil Jackson*

"Before we acquire great power we must acquire wisdom to use it well."

— *Ralph Waldo Emerson*

"Wonder is the beginning of wisdom."

— *Socrates*

"Nearly all men can stand adversity, but if you want to test a man's character, give him power."

— *Abraham Lincoln*

"Reading is to the mind, as exercise is to the body."

— *Brian Tracy*

"The man who does not read has no advantage over the man who cannot read."
— *Mark Twain*

"A reader lives a thousand lives before he dies. The man who never reads lives only one."
— *George R.R. Martin*

"For every reason it's not possible, there are a hundred of people who have faced the same circumstances and succeeded."
— *Jack Canfield*

"To know even one life has breathed easier because you have lived. This is to have succeeded."
— *Ralph Waldo Emerson*

"Things work out best for those who make the best of how things work out."
— *John Wooden*

"A room without books is like a body without a soul."
— *Marcus Tullius Cicero*

"There are essentially two things that will make you wise, the books you read and the people you meet."
— *Jack Canfield*

"There are two things a person should never be angry at, what they can help, and what they cannot."
— *Plato*

"Never answer a letter while you are angry."
— *Chinese proverb*

"I think goals should never be easy, they should force you to work, even if they are uncomfortable at the time."
— *Michael Phelps*

"If you're too comfortable, it's time to move on. Terrified of what's next? You're on the right track."
— *Susan Fales-Hill*

"You don't have to be great to start, but you have to start to be great."
— *Zig Ziglar*

"Study while others are sleeping, work while others are loafing, prepare while others are playing; and dream while others are wishing."
— *William Arthur Ward*

"Before beginning, prepare carefully."
— *Marcus Tullius Cicero*

"The Chinese use two brush strokes to write the word 'crisis.' One brush stroke stands for danger; the other for opportunity. In a crisis, be aware of the danger–but recognize the opportunity."
— *John F. Kennedy*

"Opportunity often comes disguised in the form of misfortune or temporary defeat."
— *Napoleon Hill*

"The harder you work, the luckier you get."
— *Mike Adenuga*

"A clear vision, backed by definite plans, gives you a tremendous feeling of confidence and personal power."
— *Brian Tracy*

"Books and published works offer the most in term of documented research and role models for success."
— *Gary Keller*

"There are really only three types of people: those who make things happen, those who watch things happen, and those who say, What happened?"
— *Ann Landers*

"The people who get on in this world are the people who get up and look for the circumstance they want and, if they can't find them, make them."

— *George Bernard Shaw*

"There is little difference in people......the little difference is attitude. The big difference is whether it is positive or negative."

— *Clement Stone*

"A bad attitude is like a flat tire, you can't get very far until you change it."

— *Unknown*

"Begin it, and the work will be completed."

— *Johann Wolfgang von Goethe*

"Whenever you see a successful business, someone once made a courageous decision."

— *Peter Drucker*

"Business is like riding a bicycle. Either you keep moving or you fall down."

— *John David Wright*

"Master a trade, and God will provide."

— *Midrash*

"I believe that the true road to per-eminent success in any line is to make yourself master of that line."

— *Andrew Carnegie*

"Poor is the pupil who does not surpass his master."

— *Leonardo da Vinci*

"Success can be attained in any branch of labor. There's always room at the top in every pursuit."

— *Andrew Carnegie*

"First say to yourself what you would be; and then do what you have to do."
— *Epictetus*

"When possible, make the decisions now, even if action is in the future. A reviewed decision usually is better than one reached at the last moment."
— *William B. Given, Jr.*

"If today you are a little better than you were yesterday, then that's enough."
— *David A. Bednar*

"You were born to be a player. You were meant to be here. This moment is yours."
— *Herb Brooks*

"Often greater risk is involved in postponement than in making a wrong decision."
— *Harry A. Hopf*

"Once you make a decision, the universe conspires to make it happen."
— *Ralph Waldo Emerson*

"No man is able of himself to do all things."
— *Homer*

"Few things are impossible to diligence and skill… Great works are performed, not by strength, but perseverance."
— *Samuel Johnson*

"If it doesn't challenge you, it doesn't change you."
— *Fred DeVito*

"There are no gains without pains."
— *Benjamin Franklin*

"Everything is hard before it is easy."
— *Johann Wolfgang von Goethe*

"It's a rare person who doesn't get discouraged. Whether it happens to us or to an associate we're trying to cheer up, the answer centers arounds one word: Perseverance."
— *Unknown*

"The best executive is the one who has sense enough to pick good men to do what he wants done, and self-restraint enough to keep from meddling with them while they do it."
— *Theodore Roosevelt*

"Forget your excuses. You either want it bad or don't want it at all."
— *Unknown*

"Ninety-nine percent of failures comes from people who have the habit of making excuses."
— *George Washington Carver*

"You're so much stronger than your excuses."
— *Unknown*

"A positive mind finds a way it can be done; A negative mind looks for all the ways it can't be done."
— *Napoleon Hill*

"No true and permanent fame can be found except in labors which promote the happiness of mankind."
— *Charles Sumner*

"Man is so made that he can only find relaxation from one kind of labor by taking up another."
— *Anatole France*

"Arriving at one goal is the starting point to another."
— *John Dewey*

"The glory of great men should be measured by the means they have used to acquire it."
— *La Rochefoucauld*

"The grand essentials of happiness are: something to do, something to love, and something to hope for."
— *Allan K. Chalmers*

"Happiness lies, first of all, in health."
— *George William Curtis*

"The greatest mistake a man can make is to sacrifice health for any other advantage."
— *Arthur Pierce Adams*

"It is impossible to enjoy idling thoroughly, unless one has plenty of work to do."
— *Jerome K. Jerome*

"Everything comes to him who hustles while he waits."
— *Thomas A. Edison*

"Fortune sides with him who dares."
— *Virgil*

"Intuition is reason in a hurry."
— *Holbrook Jackson*

"Intuition will tell the thinking mind where to look next."
— *Jonas Salk*

"The secret of life is not to do what you like, but to like what you do."
— *Unknown*

"Success is liking yourself, liking what you do, and how you do it."
— *Maya Angelou*

"Shallow men believe in luck. Strong men believe in cause and effect."
— *Ralph Waldo Emerson*

"I shall argue that strong men conversely know when to compromise and that all principles can be compromised to serve a greater purpose."
— *Andrew Carnegie*

"Luck is what happens when preparation meets opportunity."
— *Seneca*

"I believe that people make their own luck by great preparation and good strategy."
— *Jack Canfield*

"Some luck lies in not getting what you thought you wanted but getting what you have, which once you have got it you may be smart enough to see is what you would have wanted had you known."
— *Garrison Keillor*

"Success depends on previous preparation, and without such preparation there is sure to be failure."
— *Confucius*

"If you fail to prepare, you're prepared to fail."
— *Mark Spitz*

"The will to win is important, but the will to prepare is vital."
— *Joe Paterno*

"Ask and it will be given to you; seek and you will find it, knock and the door will opened to you."
— *Matthew 7:7*

"If you cannot do great things, do small things in a great way."
— *Napoleon Hill*

"You get in life what you have the courage to ask for."
— *Nancy D. Solomon*

"Everything you want is out there waiting for you to ask. Everything you want also wants you. But you have to take action to get it."
— *Jack Canfield*

"We are Divine enough to ask, and we are important enough to receive."
— *Wayne Dyer*

"All our dreams can come true, if we have the courage to pursue them."
— *Walt Disney*

"When you know what you want, and want it bad enough, you'll find a way to get it."
— *Jim Rohn*

"Setting goals is the first step into turning the invisible into the visible."
— *Anthony Robbins*

"Vague goals produce vague results."
— *Jack Canfield*

"Believe in yourself. You are braver than you think, more talented than you know, and capable of more than you imagine."
— *Roy T. Bennett*

"Once you believe in yourself and see your soul as divine and precious, you'll automatically be converted to a being who can create miracles."
— *Wayne Dyer*

"Your mind is a powerful thing. When you fill it with positive thought, your life will start to change."
— *Unknown*

"No man is free who is not master of himself."
— *Epictetus*

"The two most important days in your life are the day you are born and the day you find out why."
— *Mark Twain*

"The future belongs to those who believe in the beauty of their dreams."
— *Eleanor Roosevelt*

"Planning is bringing the future into the present so that you can do something about it now."
— *Alan Lakein*

"Go for it now. The future is promised to no one."
— *Wayne Dyer*

"To see things in the seed, that is genius."
— *Lao-Tzu*

"Everything you've ever wanted is on the other side of fear."
— *George Addair*

"Fear not, for I am with you; be not dismayed, for I am your God; I will strengthen you, I will help you, I will uphold you with my righteous right hand."
— *Isaiah 41:10*

"Keep your mind fixed on what you want in life: not on what you don't want."
— *Napoleon Hill*

"Decide what you want, believe you can have it, believe you deserve it and believe it's possible for you."
— *Jack Canfield*

"Believe you can and you will."
— *Unknown*

"Too many of us are not living our dreams because we are living our fears."
— *Les Brown*

"To be a star, you must shine your own light, follow your own path, and don't worry about darkness, for that is when the stars shine brightest."
— *Napoleon Hill*

"Remember, today is the tomorrow you worried about yesterday."
— *Dale Carnegie*

"If you can dream it, then you can achieve it. You will get all you want in life if you help enough people get what they want."
— *Zig Ziglar*

"One of the most beautiful compensations in life is that no person can help another without helping themselves."
— *Ralph Waldo Emerson*

"There is no use whatever trying to help people who do not help themselves. You cannot push anyone up a ladder unless he be willing to climb himself."
— *Andrew Carnegie*

"I cannot teach anybody anything, I can only make them think."
— *Socrates*

"Always do your best. What you plant now, you will harvest later."
— *Og Mandino*

"Nobody who ever gave their best regretted it."
— *George Halas*

"When you want to succeed as bad as you want to breathe, then you'll be successful."
— *Eric Thomas*

"If you are going to be successful in creating the life of your dreams, you first have to believe what you want is possible and you are capable of making it happen."
— *Jack Canfield*

"We are all here for some special reason. Stop being a prisoner of your past. Become the architect of your future."
— *Robin Sharma*

"You become what you think about all day long."
— *Ralph Waldo Emerson*

"Not only do you become what you think about, but the world also becomes what you think about. Those who think that the world is a dark place are blind to the light that might illuminate their lives. Those who see the light of the world view the dark spots as merely potential light."
— *Wayne Dyer*

"Follow your hunches like the ancient navigators followed the stars. The voyage may be lonely, but the stars will take you where you want to go."
— *David J. Mahoney*

"Nothing is so well learned as that which is discovered."
— *Socrates*

"Great discoveries and improvements invariably involve the cooperation of many minds. I may be given credit for having blazed the trail but when I look at the subsequent developments, I feel the credit is due to others rather than myself."
— *Alexander Graham Bell*

"They that govern the most make the least noise."
— *John Selden*

"Keep your fears to yourself, but share your courage with others."
— *Robert Louis Stevenson*

"Good management consists in showing average people how to do the work of superior people."
— *John D. Rockefeller, Sr.*

"Maturity is the capacity to endure uncertainty."
— *John Finley*

"Great men have been characterized by the greatness of their mistakes as well as by the greatness of their achievements."
— *Abraham Myerson*

"The darkest hour of any man's life is when he sits down to plan how to get money without earning it."
— *Horace Greeley*

"A good name is rather to be chosen than great riches."
— *Proverbs 22:1*

"A person's name is to that person the sweetest and most important sound in any language."
— *Dale Carnegie*

"Remember a name and call it easily and you have paid a subtle and very effective compliment."
— *Dale Carnegie*

"Necessity makes even the timid brave."
— *Sallust*

"Restlessness and discontent are the first necessities of progress."
— *Thomas A. Edison*

"When I'm getting ready to reason with a man I spend one-third of my time thinking about myself and what I am going to say---and two-thirds thinking about him and what he is going to say."
— *Abraham Lincoln*

"A wise man will make more opportunities than he finds."
— *Francis Bacon*

"The wise man put all his eggs in one basket and watches the basket."
— *Andrew Carnegie*

"A hero is born among a hundred, a wise man is found among a thousand, but an accomplished one might not be found even among a hundred thousand men."

— *Plato*

"Don't sit down and wait for the opportunities to come. Get up and make them."

— *Madame C. J. Walker*

"A friendship founded on business is better than a business founded on friendship."

— *John D. Rockefeller, Jr.*

"Friendship, like the immortality of the soul, is too good to be believed."

— *Ralph Waldo Emerson*

"So long as there is breath in me, that long will I persist. For now I know one of the greatest principles of success; if I persist long enough I will win."

— *Og Mandino*

"The men who have succeeded are men who have chosen one line and stuck to it."

— *Andrew Carnegie*

"Persistence is probably the single most common quality of high achievers. They simply refuse to give up. The longer you hang in there, the greater the chance that something will happen in your favor. No matter how hard it seems, the longer you persist the more likely your success."

— *Jack Canfield*

"Patience, persistence and perspiration make an unbeatable combination for success."

— *Napoleon Hill*

"The poor have to work so hard making a living, they haven't time to get rich."

— *Unknown*

"Action may not always bring happiness, but there is no happiness without action."

— *Benjamin Disraeli*

"The mark of a great man is one who know when to set aside the important things in order to accomplish the vital one."

— *Brandon Sanderson*

"He is strong who conquers others; he who conquers himself is mighty."

— *Lao-Tzu*

"I cannot trust a man to control others who cannot control himself."

— *Robert E. Lee*

"Without self-discipline, success is impossible, period."

— *Lou Holtz*

"In the end, it is important to remember that we cannot become what we need to be by remaining what we are."

— *Max De Pree*

"Show me the man you honor and I will know what kind of man you are."

— *Thomas John Carlisle*

"Do the right thing even when no one is looking."

— *Unknown*

"Integrity means honesty and willingness to fulfil a promise, even at high cost."

— *Morris Chang*

"The most virtuous are those who content themselves with being virtuous without seeking to appear so."
— *Plato*

"There are men and women who make the world better just by being the kind of people they are. They have the gift of kindness or courage or loyalty or integrity. It really matters very little whether they are behind the wheel of a truck or running a business or bringing up a family. They teach the truth by living it."
— *James Garfield*

"The greatest gift is a portion of thyself."
— *Ralph Waldo Emerson*

"We can see through others only when we can see through ourselves."
— *Bruce Lee*

"Honesty is the first chapter of the book wisdom."
— *Thomas Jefferson*

"Honesty is for the most part less profitable than dishonesty."
— *Plato*

"Procrastination is the bad habit of putting off until the day after tomorrow what should have been done yesterday."
— *Napoleon Hill*

"Procrastination is the thief of time."
— *Edward Young*

"Today is your opportunity to build the tomorrow you want."
— *Ken Poirot*

"There can be no security for any employee in any business that doesn't make money. There can be no growth for that business. There can be no opportunity for the individual to achieve his personal ambitions unless his company makes money."
— *Duncan C. Manzies*

"I quote others only the better to express myself."
— *Michel de Montaigne*

"Quotations when engraved upon the memory give you good thoughts."
— *Winston Churchill*

"He that loves reading has everything within his reach."
— *William Godwin*

"Nothing is more futile than doing your best using an approach that can't deliver results equal to your efforts."
— *Gary Keller*

"Always make a total effort, even when the odds are against you."
— *Arnold Palmer*

"When you hire people who are smarter than you are, you prove you are smarter than they are."
— *Robert H. Grant*

"To climb steep hills requires slow pace at first."
— *William Shakespeare*

"He who toils with pain will eat with pleasure."
— *Chinese Proverb*

"What hurts you blesses you."
— *Rumi*

"The woman who follows the crowd will usually go no further than the crowd. The woman who walks alone is likely to find herself in places no one has been before."
— *Albert Einstein*

"It takes nothing to join the crowd. It takes everything to stand alone."
— *Hans F. Hansen*

"Society demands conformity at the expense of individual liberty. Let us be for once a non-conformist to be fully alive."
— *Wayne Dyer*

"Always be careful when you follow the masses. Sometimes the m is silent."
— *Unknown*

"The most difficult part of getting to the top of the ladder is getting through the crowd at the bottom."
— *Arch Ward*

"The ladder of success is never crowded at the top."
— *Napoleon Hill*

"When sorrows come, they come not as single spies, But in battalions!"
— *William Shakespeare*

"Time on a task, over time, eventually beats talent every time."
— *Garry Keller*

"Life is a journey, not a destination."
— *Ralph Waldo Emerson*

"One half of knowing what you want is knowing what you must give up before you get it."
— *Sidney Howard*

"You give before you get."
— *Napoleon Hill*

"The brave man is not he who does not feel afraid, but he who conquers that fear."
— *Nelson Mandela*

"People are always blaming circumstances for what they are. I don't believe in circumstances. The people who get on in this world are the people who get fed up and look for the circumstances they want, and if they can't find them, make them."
— *George Bernard Shaw*

"Wise men put their trust in ideas and not in circumstances."
— *Ralph Waldo Emerson*

"Our words must be judged by our deeds, and if we cannot attain all at one leap, we must advance towards it step by step, reasonably content so long as we do actually make some progress in the right direction."
— *Theodore Roosevelt*

"Fate is nothing but the deeds committed in a prior state of existence."
— *Ralph Waldo Emerson*

"Great deeds are usually wrought at great risks."
— *Herodotus*

"It's a fact of life that progress is almost exclusively generated through people. If you're not sensitive to the needs of people within your organization, or with whom you have to deal, you're not going to be effective."
— *Reginald F. Lewis*

"To do the useful thing, to say the courageous thing, to contemplate the beautiful thing that is enough for one man's life."
— *Thomas Stearns*

"The reward of a thing well done is having done it."
— *Ralph Waldo Emerson*

"It's up to you to bring yourself to the attention of powerful people around you. They're not going to find you on their own."
— *Richard Parsons*

"Success is to be measured not so much by the position that one has reached in life as by the obstacles which he has overcome while trying to succeed."
— Booker T. Washington

"If you believe it'll work out, you'll see opportunities. If you don't believe it'll work out you'll see obstacles."
— Wayne Dyer

"Magic is believing in yourself, if you can do that, you can make anything happen."
— Johann Wolfgang von Goethe

"Don't wish it were easier. Wish you were better."
— Jim Rohn

"You don't-need to be better than anyone else you just need to be better than you used to be."
— Wayne Dyer

"Decide upon your major definite purpose in life and then organize all your activities around it."
— Brian Tracy

"When you are inspired by some great purpose, some extraordinary project, all your thoughts break their bonds."
— Patanjali

"When you have inspired thought, you have to trust it and you have to act on it."
— Jack Canfield

"Your mind is a powerful thing. When you fill it with positive thoughts, your life will start to change."
— Unknown

"The state of your life is nothing more than a reflection of the state of your mind."
 — *Wayne Dyer*

"You have to be odd to be number one."
 — *Dr. Seuss*

"You'll never change your life until you change something you do daily. The secret of your success is found in your daily routine."
 — *John C. Maxwell*

"You have the power to achieve greatness and create anything and everything you want in life, but you have to take action."
 — *Jack Canfield*

"Take action, an inch of movement will bring you closer to your goals than a mile of intention."
 — *Steve Maraboli*

"I believe that the only courage anybody ever needs is the courage to follow your own dreams."
 — *Oprah Winfrey.*

"Do the difficult things while they are easy and do the great things while they are small. A journey of a thousand miles must begin with a single step."
 — *Lao-Tzu*

"Every artist was first an amateur."
 — *Ralph Waldo Emerson*

"No man has the right to be an amateur in the matter of physical training. It is a shame for a man to grow old without seeing the beauty and strength of which his body is capable."
 — *Socrates*

"You cannot push anyone up a ladder unless he is willing to climb a little."

— *Andrew Carnegie*

"Before you speak, listen. Before you write, think. Before you spend, earn. Before you invest, investigate. Before you criticize, wait. Before you pray, forgive. Before you quit, try. Before you retire, save. Before you die, give."

— *William A. Ward*

"Listen with the intent to understand, not the intent to reply."

— *Stephen Covey*

"Think twice before you speak, because your words and influence will plant the seed of either success or failure in the mind of another."

— *Napoleon Hill*

"Forgive your enemies, but never forget their names."

— *John F. Kennedy*

"It is not the man who has too little, but the man who craves more, that is poor."

— *Seneca*

"Money is only a tool. It will take you wherever you wish, but it will not replace you as the driver."

— *Ayn Rand*

"Be as you wish to seem."

— *Socrates*

"Learn to light a candle in the darkest moments of someone's life. Be the light that helps others see, it is what gives life its deepest significance."

— *Roy T. Bennett*

"Not he who has much is rich, but he who gives much."

— *Erich Fromm*

"The more you give, the more comes back to you."
— *Napoleon Hill*

"True perfection is a bold quest to seek. Only the willing and true of heart will seek the betterment of many."
— *Socrates*

"Don't stay in bed unless you can make money in bed."
— *George Burns*

"Time is more valuable than money. You can get more money, but you cannot get more time."
— *Jim Rohn*

"The person who doesn't know where his next dollar is coming from usually doesn't know where his last dollar went."
— *Unknown*

"It doesn't matter about money; having it, not having it. Or having clothes, or not having them. You're still left alone with yourself in the end."
— *Billy Idol*

"Money does not buy you happiness, but lack of money certainly buys you misery."
— *Daniel Kahneman*

"Ask yourself: What is the worst that can happen? Then prepare to accept it. Then proceed to improve on the worst."
— *Dale Carnegie*

"It's not the will to win that matters—everyone has that. It's the will to prepare to win that matters."
— *Paul "Bear" Bryant*

"Expect the best. Prepare for the worst. Capitalize on what comes."
— *Zig Ziglar*

"It's good to have money and the things that money can buy, but it's good, too, to check up once in a while and make sure that you haven't lost the things that money can't buy."
— *George Lorimer*

"I don't pay good wages because I have a lot of money; I have a lot of money because I pay good wages."
— *Robert Bosch*

"Making money is a common sense. It's not rocket science. But unfortunately, when it comes to money, common sense is uncommon."
— *Robert Kiyosaki*

"Money is like love; it kills slowly and painfully the one who withholds it, and enlivens the other who turns it on his fellow man."
— *Kahlil Gibran*

"It is a kind of spiritual snobbery that makes people think they can be happy without money."
— *Albert Camus*

"The money you have gives you freedom; the money you pursue enslaves you."
— *Jean-Jacques Rousseau*

"Money is like muck—not good unless it be spread."
— *Francis Bacon*

"It's not the employer who pays the wages. Employers only handle the money. It's the customer who pays the wages."
— *Henry Ford*

"Money is multiplied in practical value depending on the number of W's you control in your life: what you do, when you do it, where you do it, and with whom you do it."
— *Tim Ferriss*

"If you would be wealthy, think of saving as well as getting."
— *Ben Franklin*

"Capital as such is not evil; it is its wrong use that is evil. Capital in some form or other will always be needed."
— *Mahatma Gandhi*

"They deem me mad because I will not sell my days for gold; and I deem them mad because they think my days have a price."
— *Kahlil Gibran*

"I made my money the old-fashioned way. I was very nice to a wealthy relative right before he died."
— *Malcolm Forbes*

"If we command our wealth, we shall be rich and free. If our wealth commands us, we are poor indeed."
— *Edmund Burke*

"When a fellow says it ain't the money but the principle of the thing, it's the money."
— *Artemus Ward*

"Wealth is like sea-water; the more we drink, the thirstier we become; and the same is true of fame."
— *Arthur Schopenhauer*

"The real measure of your wealth is how much you'd be worth if you lost all your money."
— *Unknown*

"He who loses money, loses much; He who loses a friend, loses much more; He who loses faith, loses all."
— *Eleanor Roosevelt*

"Happiness is not in the mere possession of money; it lies in the joy of achievement, in the thrill of creative effort."
— *Franklin D. Roosevelt*

"To acquire money requires valor, to keep money requires prudence, and to spend money well is an art."
— *Berthold Auerbach*

"Money is good for nothing unless you know the value of it by experience."
— *P.T. Barnum*

"Tell me how you use your spare time, and how you spend your money, and I will tell you where and what you will be in ten years from now."
— *Napoleon Hill*

"Never spend your money before you have earned it."
— *Thomas Jefferson*

"The habit of saving is itself an education; it fosters every virtue, teaches self-denial, cultivates the sense of order, trains to forethought, and so broadens the mind."
— *T.T. Munger*

"Money may not buy happiness, but I'd rather cry in a Jaguar than on a bus."
— *Francoise Sagan*

"Many folks think they aren't good at earning money, when what they don't know is how to use it."
— *Frank A. Clark*

"Many people take no care of their money till they come nearly to the end of it, and others do just the same with their time."
— *Johann Wolfgang von Goethe*

"Never stand begging for that which you have the power to earn."
— *Miguel de Cervantes*

"I pity that man who wants a coat so cheap that the man or woman who produces the cloth shall starve in the process."
— *Benjamin Harrison*

"Empty pockets never held anyone back. Only empty heads and empty hearts can do that."

— *Norman Vincent Peale*

"If you want to know what a man is really like, take notice of how he acts when he loses money."

— *Simone Weil*

"A wise person should have money in their head, but not in their heart."

— *Jonathan Swift*

"Money never made a man happy yet, nor will it. There is nothing in its nature to produce happiness. The more a man has, the more he wants. Instead of filling a vacuum, it makes one."

— *Benjamin Franklin*

"Wealth is not about having a lot of money; it's about having a lot of options."

— *Chris Rock*

"Wealth is the ability to fully experience life."

— *Henry David Thoreau*

"A simple fact that is hard to learn is that the time to save money is when you have some."

— *Joe Moore*

"Know what you own, and know why you own it."

— *Peter Lynch*

"Money isn't everything…but it ranks right up there with oxygen."

— *Rita Davenport*

"You can only become truly accomplished at something you love. Don't make money your goal. Instead, pursue the things you love doing, and then do them so well that people can't take their eyes off you."

— *Maya Angelou*

"Don't tell me where your priorities are. Show me where you spend your money and I'll tell you what they are."
— *James W. Frick*

"Buy when everyone else is selling and hold until everyone else is buying. That's not just a catchy slogan. It's the very essence of successful investing."
— *J. Paul Getty*

"If you don't value your time, neither will others. Stop giving away your time and talents. Value what you know and start charging for it."
— *Kim Garst*

"If money is your hope for independence you will never have it. The only real security that a man will have in this world is a reserve of knowledge, experience, and ability."
— *Henry Ford*

"Every time you borrow money, you're robbing your future self."
— *Nathan W. Morris*

"Investing should be more like watching paint dry or watching grass grow. If you want excitement, take $800 and go to Las Vegas."
— *Paul Samuelson*

"There is only one boss. The customer. And he can fire everybody in the company from the chairman on down, simply by spending his money somewhere else."
— *Sam Walton*

"Success is not the result of making money; earning money is the result of success – and success is in direct proportion to our service."
— *Earl Nightingale*

"If you want to get rich, remember that the way to do it is via equity, not salary."
— *Sam Altman*

"No wealth can ever make a bad man at peace with himself."
— *Plato*

"There are a great many people accumulating what they think is vast wealth, but it's only money."
— *Alan Watts*

"It's simple arithmetic: "Your income can grow only to the extent you do."
— *T. Harv Eker*

"Success isn't always about greatness. It's about consistent hard work leads to success. Greatness will come."
— *Dwane Johnson*

"Wealth does not make people happy, but positive increases in wealth may."
— *Nassim Nicholas Taleb*

"Spend your money on the things money can buy. Spend your time on the things money can't buy."
— *Haruki Murakami*

"Remember that the only purpose of money is to get you what you want, so think hard about what you value and put it above money."
— *Ray Dalio*

"Wealth after all is a relative thing since he that has little and wants less is richer than he that has much and wants more."
— *Charles Caleb Colton*

"Within certain limits, it is actually true that the less money you have, the less you worry."
— *George Orwell*

"The four most expensive words in the English language are, 'This time it's different."
— *Sir John Templeton*

"Be careful to leave your sons well instructed rather than rich, for the hopes of the instructed are better than the wealth of the ignorant."
— *Epictetus*

"Money grows on the tree of persistence."
— *Japanese proverb*

"Persistence can change failure into extraordinary achievement."
— *Marv Levy*

"I think everybody should get rich and famous and do everything they ever dreamed of so they can see that it's not the answer."
— *Jim Carrey*

"Real wealth is not about money. Real wealth is: not having to go to meetings, not having to spend time with jerks, not being locked into status games, not feeling like you have to say "yes", not worrying about others claiming your time and energy. Real wealth is about freedom."
— *James Clear*

"If you can't sleep, then get up and do something instead of lying there and worrying. It's the worry that gets you, not the loss of sleep."
— *Dale Carnegie*

"Try to save something while your salary is small; it's impossible to save after you begin to earn more."
— *Jack Benny*

"The rich invest their money and spend what is left; the poor spend their money and invest what is left."
— *Jim Rohn*

"How many millionaires do you know who have become wealthy by investing in savings accounts? I rest my case."
— *Robert G. Allen*

"So many people of wealth understand much more about making and saving money than about using and enjoying it. They fail to live because they are always preparing to live."
— *Alan Watts*

"Stop buying things you don't need, to impress people you don't even like."
— *Suze Orman*

"One reason why birds and horses are not unhappy is because they are not trying to impress other birds and horses."
— *Dale Carnegie*

"Wealth is not his that has it, but his that enjoys it."
— *Benjamin Franklin*

"It's easy to say you don't care about money when you have plenty of it."
— *Ransom Riggs*

"In the Middle Ages, the rich spent their money carelessly on extravagant luxuries, whereas peasants lived frugally minding every penny. Today, the tables have turned. The rich take great care managing their assets and investments while the less well go into debt buying cars and televisions they don't really need."
— *Yuval Noah Harari*

"Money moves from those who do not manage it to those who do."
— *Dave Ramsey*

"If you cannot control your emotions, you cannot control your money."
— *Warren Buffett*

"It's not how much money you make, but how much money you keep, how hard it works for you, and how many generations you keep it for."
— *Robert Kiyosaki*

"You must gain control over your money or the lack of it will forever control you."

— *Dave Ramsey*

"Success is most often achieved by those who don't know that failure is inevitable."

— *Coco Chanel*

"Courage is grace under pressure."

— *Ernest Hemingway*

"Learn from yesterday, live for today, hope for tomorrow. The important thing is not to stop questioning."

— *Albert Einstein*

"Take up one idea. Make that one idea your life -- think of it, dream of it, live on that idea. Let the brain, muscles, nerves, every part of your body be full of that idea, and just leave every other idea alone. This is the way to success."

— *Swami Vivekananda*

"Whenever you see a successful person, you only see the public glories, never the private sacrifices to reach them."

— *Vaibhav Shah*

"Once you choose hope, anything's possible."

— *Christopher Reeve*

"There is no easy walk to freedom anywhere, and many of us will have to pass through the valley of the shadow of death again and again before we reach the mountaintop of our desires."

— *Nelson Mandela*

"It is not the strongest of the species that survive, nor the most intelligent, but the one most responsive to change."

— *Charles Darwin*

"I know that I am intelligent because I know that I know nothing."
— *Socrates*

"If you can't do anything about it then let it go. Don't be a prisoner to things you can't change."
— *Tony Gaskins*

"Live as if you were to die tomorrow. Learn as if you were to live forever."
— *Mahatma Gandhi*

"The best revenge is massive success."
— *Frank Sinatra*

"Revenge is a powerful motivator."
— *Marcus Luttrell*

"I am thankful for all of those who said NO to me. It's because of them I'm doing it myself."
— *Unknown*

"When you feel like giving up just remember that there are a lot of people you still have to prove wrong."
— *Unknown*

"You can't win an argument. If you lose it, you lose it; and if you win it, you lose it. There is only one way to get the best of an argument -- and that is to avoid it."
— *Dale Carnegie*

"The difference between winning and losing is most often not quitting."
— *Walt Disney*

"Failure is another steppingstone to greatness."
— *Oprah Winfrey*

"If you're not stubborn, you'll give up on experiments too soon. And if you're not flexible, you'll pound your head against the wall and you won't see a different solution to a problem you're trying to solve."
— *Jeff Bezos*

"In order to be irreplaceable one must always be different."
— *Coco Chanel*

"Strength lies in differences, not in similarities."
— *Stephen Covey*

"What seems to us as bitter trials are often blessings in disguise."
— *Oscar Wilde*

"The distance between insanity and genius is measured only by success."
— *Bruce Feirstein*

"The way I see it, if you want the rainbow, you gotta put up with the rain."
— *Dolly Parton*

"To me, business isn't about wearing suits or pleasing stockholders. It's about being true to yourself, your ideas and focusing on the essentials."
— *Sir. Richard Branson*

"Happiness is a butterfly, which when pursued, is always beyond your grasp, but which, if you will sit down quietly, may alight upon you."
— *Nathaniel Hawthorne*

"You must expect great things of yourself before you can do them."
— *Michael Jordan*

"If you can't explain it simply, you don't understand it well enough."
— *Albert Einstein*

"You can't please everyone, and you can't make everyone like you."
— *Katie Couric*

"Be nicer than necessary to everyone you meet. Everyone is fighting some kind of battle."

— *Socrates*

"I believe every human has a finite number of heartbeats. I don't intend to waste any of mine."

— *Neil Armstrong*

"Start where you are. Use what you have. Do what you can."

— *Arthur Ashe*

"Don't wait. The time will never be just right. Start where you stand, and work whatever tools you may have at your command and better tools will be found as you go along."

— *Napoleon Hill*

"I find that the harder I work, the more luck I seem to have."

— *Thomas Jefferson*

"It often requires more courage to dare to do right than to fear to do wrong."

— *Abraham Lincoln*

"Success is the sum of small efforts, repeated day-in and day-out."

— *Robert Collier*

"As you grow older, you will discover that you have two hands, one for helping yourself, the other for helping others."

— *Audrey Hepburn*

"It is literally true that you can succeed best and quickest by helping others succeed."

— *Napoleon Hill*

"If you want to achieve excellence, you can get there today. As of this second, quit doing less-than-excellent work."

— *Thomas J. Watson*

"If your actions inspire others to dream more, learn more, do more, and become more, you are a leader."

— *John Quincy Adams*

"The more you praise and celebrate your life, the more there is in life to celebrate."

— *Oprah Winfrey*

"You may only succeed if you desire succeeding; you may only fail if you do not mind failing."

— *Philippos*

"A dream doesn't become reality through magic; it takes sweat, determination, and hard work."

— *Colin Powell*

"Some people dream of success, while others wake up and work hard at it."

— *Napoleon Hill*

"Only put off until tomorrow what you are willing to die having left undone."

— *Pablo Picasso*

"We become what we think about most of the time, and that's the strangest secret."

— *Earl Nightingale*

"Don't be afraid to give up the good to go for the great."

— *John D. Rockefeller, Jr.*

"Though no one can go back and make a brand-new start, anyone can start from now and make a brand-new ending."

— *Carl Bard*

"Twenty years from now you will be more disappointed by the things that you didn't do than by the ones you did do. So throw off the bowlines. Sail away from the safe harbor. Catch the trade winds in your sails. Explore. Dream. Discover."
— *Mark Twain*

"One of the greatest diseases is to be nobody to anybody."
— *Mother Teresa*

"Identity is a prison you can never escape, but the way to redeem your past is not to run from it, but to try to understand it, and use it as a foundation to grow."
— *Jay-Z*

"Rarely have I seen a situation where doing less than the other guy is a good strategy."
— *Jimmy Spithill*

"You can't connect the dots looking forward; you can only connect them looking backward. So you have to trust that the dots will somehow connect in your future. You have to trust in something -- your gut, destiny, life, karma, whatever. This approach has never let me down, and it has made all the difference in my life."
— *Steve Jobs*

"Everything you can imagine is real."
— *Pablo Picasso*

"If you talk about it, it's a dream. If you envision it, it's possible. If you schedule it, it's real."
— *Anthony Robbins*

"If you want to make a permanent change, stop focusing on the size of your problems and start focusing on the size of you!"
— *T. Harv Eker*

"When you show deep empathy toward others, their defensive energy goes down, and positive energy replaces it. That's when you can get more creative in solving problems."
— *Stephen Covey*

"Talk to someone about themselves and they'll listen for hours."
— *Dale Carnegie*

"If you love what you do and are willing to do what it takes, it's within your reach. And it'll be worth every minute you spend alone at night, thinking and thinking about what it is you want to design or build."
— *Steve Wozniak*

"Doing what you love is the cornerstone of having abundance in your life."
— *Wayne Dyer*

"In my experience, there is only one motivation, and that is desire. No reasons or principle contain it or stand against it."
— *Jane Smiley*

"In the midst of movement and chaos, keep stillness inside of you."
— *Deepak Chopra*

"If you want to fly give up everything that weights you down."
— *Buddha*

"Success does not consist in never making mistakes but in never making the same one a second time."
— *George Bernard Shaw*

"I choose to make the rest of my life, the best of my life."
— *Louise Hay*

"I don't want to get to the end of my life and find that I lived just the length of it. I want to have lived the width of it as well."
— *Diane Ackerman*

"As we look ahead into the next century, leaders will be those who empower others."
    — *Bill Gates*

"But you have to do what you dream of doing even while you're afraid."
    — *Arianna Huffington*

"To be successful, you must accept all challenges that come your way. You can't just accept the ones you like."
    — *Mike Gafka*

"Go the extra mile, it's never crowded there."
    — *Wayne Dyer*

"People are more likely to accept an order if they had a part in the decision that caused the order to be issued."
    — *Dale Carnegie*

"Be patient with yourself. Self-growth is tender; it's holy ground. There's no greater investment."
    — *Stephen Covey*

"The greatest wealth is to live content with little."
    — *Plato*

"He is rich who is content with the least; for contentment is the wealth of nature."
    — *Socrates*

"A wise man is content with his lot, whatever it may be, without wishing for what he has not."
    — *Seneca*

"He who is not contented with what he has, would not be contented with what he would like to have."
    — *Socrates*

"Our life is what our thoughts make it."
> — *Marcus Aurelius*

"The greatest weapon against stress is the ability to choose one thought over another."
> — *William James*

"Good is not good when better is expected."
> — *Vin Scully*

"How wonderful it is that nobody needs to wait a single moment before starting to improve the world."
> — *Anne Frank*

"Self-interest demands that you be interested in the well-being of others."
> — *B.C. Forbes*

"Pleasure in the job puts perfection in the work."
> — *Aristotle*

"Some women choose to follow men, and some women choose to follow their dreams. If you're wondering which way to go, remember that your career will never wake up and tell you that it doesn't love you anymore."
> — *Lady Gaga*

"If you don't get out of the box you've been raised in, you won't understand how much bigger the world is."
> — *Angelina Jolie*

"Here are the crazy ones. The misfits. The rebels. The troublemakers. The round pegs in the square holes. The ones who see things differently. They're not fond of rules. And they have no respect for the status quo. You can quote them, disagree with them, glorify or vilify them. About the only thing you can't do is ignore them. Because they change things. They push the human race forward. And while some may see them as the crazy ones, we see genius. Because the people who are crazy enough to think they can change the world, are the ones who do."

— *Rob Siltanen*

"Men of lofty genius when they are doing the least work are most active."

— *Leonardo da Vinci*

"To learn a language is to have one more window from which to look at the world."

— *Chinese Proverb*

"Everything you need you already have. You are complete right now, you are a whole, total person, not an apprentice person on the way to someplace else. Your completeness must be understood by you and experienced in your thoughts as your own personal reality."

— *Wayne Dyer*

"Therefore I say unto you, What things soever ye desire, when ye pray, believe that ye receive them, and ye shall have them."

— *Mark 11:24*

*Are you a millionaire or multi-millionaire?
Do you want to become a billionaire?*

LET US COACH YOU!

Reach out with inquiries:

info@billionairewannabecoaching.com

Do you have an inspirational quote that you would like to offer to be included in the next edition, or an insightful or uplifting quote that you feel should be included? Do you want to purchase this book in bulk for promotional, educational, or business use? Do you want to purchase the subsidiary rights to this book?

If so, send your inquiry to: ttronck@gmail.com

www.ingramcontent.com/pod-product-compliance
Lightning Source LLC
Chambersburg PA
CBHW072042290426
44110CB00014B/1558